lust in translation

lust in translation

THE

RULES

OF

INFIDELITY

FROM

TOKYO

TO

TENNESSEE

pamela druckerman

The Penguin Press · New York · 2007

THE PENGUIN PRESS
Published by the Penguin Group
Penguin Group (USA) Inc., 375 Hudson Street, New York, New York 10014, U.S.A. • Penguin
Group (Canada), 90 Eglinton Avenue East, Suite 700, Toronto, Ontario, Canada M4P 2Y3 (a division
of Pearson Penguin Canada Inc.) • Penguin Books Ltd, 80 Strand, London WC2R 0RL, England •
Penguin Ireland, 25 St. Stephen's Green, Dublin 2, Ireland (a division of Penguin Books Ltd) •
Penguin Books Australia Ltd, 250 Camberwell Road, Camberwell, Victoria 3124, Australia (a division
of Pearson Australia Group Pty Ltd) • Penguin Books India Pvt Ltd, 11 Community Centre,
Panchsheel Park, New Delhi – 110 017, India • Penguin Group (NZ), 67 Apollo Drive, Mairangi
Bay, Auckland 1311, New Zealand (a division of Pearson New Zealand Ltd.) • Penguin Books
(South Africa) (Pty) Ltd, 24 Sturdee Avenue, Rosebank, Johannesburg 2196, South Africa

Penguin Books Ltd, Registered Offices: 80 Strand, London WC2R 0RL, England

First published in 2007 by The Penguin Press, a member of Penguin Group (USA) Inc.

The events recounted in this book are true. However, where a person is identified by first name only, the
name and some descriptive details have been changed to protect the individual's privacy.

Grateful acknowledgment is made for permission to reprint an excerpt from "Stand by Your Man,"
words and music by Tammy Wynette and Billy Sherrill. © 1968 (renewed) EMI Al Gallico Music
Corp. Worldwide print rights controlled by Alfred Publishing Co., Inc. All rights reserved. Used by
permission.

LIBRARY OF CONGRESS CATALOGING IN PUBLICATION DATA
Druckerman, Pamela.
Lust in translation : the rules of infidelity from Tokyo to Tennessee / Pamela Druckerman.
p.   cm.
ISBN 978-1-59420-114-1
1. Adultery.   2. Couples.   3. Sex.   I. Title.
HQ806.D78 2007
306.73'6—dc22   2006034996

Printed in the United States of America
1   3   5   7   9   10   8   6   4   2

Designed by Stephanie Huntwork

For Simon, for everything

Sometimes it's hard to be a woman
Giving all your love to just one man
You'll have bad times
And he'll have good times
Doing things that you don't understand.

—TAMMY WYNETTE, *Stand by Your Man*

CONTENTS

lust in translation

lust in translation

THIS IS A book about adultery. If you're American and you don't read on, I'll understand why. Adultery provokes more outrage in America than in almost any other country on record (Ireland and the Philippines are two exceptions). When I mention cheating to Americans, they usually stare at me for a few seconds, trying to sort out whether they're guilty of anything or wondering if I'm propositioning them. A few launch into rants about the importance of monogamy. Some spontaneously confess at the mere mention of infidelity.

I started seriously thinking about affairs when I was posted to Latin America for the *Wall Street Journal.* For the first time in my life, married men routinely tried to sleep with me. It wasn't, unfortunately, that I had suddenly become irresistable; many of my female friends reported similar advances. Even when these "suitors" were otherwise appealing, I found their offers repugnant. What about their obligations to their wives? I also interpreted the come-ons as personal slights. Did I seem so desperate that I'd settle for being the proverbial other woman? At the time, I was single, newly thirty, and in the market for a husband of my own.

During one such encounter, as these sanctimonious thoughts were rushing through my brain, I decided that instead of brushing off the Lothario, I'd discuss the matter with him. This particular man, the director of an Argentine beef company, had just invited me for what was obviously a romantic dinner. When I explained why I was offended by his suggestion that we casually commit adultery, he was perplexed. He said he didn't know what his wife had to do with it, since this was between us. And far from insulting me, "I am offering you great pleasure," he explained.

Although I declined his invitation, I reflected on our conversation a lot. I had imagined myself to be a cultivated woman of the world, but these men had tapped into a moralizing streak I hadn't known was there. Where did it come from? Merely by dint of having grown up in America, was I saddled with some kind of Puritan baggage that would keep me from experiencing great pleasure?

I didn't know much about affairs at the time, but it struck me that the way people in different cultures cheat—or don't cheat—reveals a lot about them. It certainly seemed to say something about me. Corruption was an open secret in Argentina, and its perpetrators among the country's elites were shameless. Politicians with modest salaries lived in fancy homes in the center of town. Magazines ran pictures of a former president's daughter on a shopping spree in Miami. The graft contributed to the collapse of the country's currency while I was there. While Argentines grumbled about corruption, many of them also seemed to understand it, and even to feel that they might do the same if given the chance. Cheating on their wives looked like part of the same package: Fidelity is a nice idea, but only fools don't grab all they can.

I was intrigued, and wanted to know more about the rules of infidelity around the world. But as I started poking around, I saw that there was no easy way to discover them in America or anyplace else. Aside from some one-liners saying the French are blasé about cheating (they aren't) or reports from anthropologists studying remote tribesmen (those thongs! who wouldn't stray?), there was very little research on the subject. Even less had been written about cheating among any of the world's middle classes. It wasn't even clear whether Americans' extreme antipathy to infidelity made them cheat any less than people in more permissive countries do.

The only way to find out how people around the world cheat was to go and ask them. So I did. I visited two dozen cities in ten countries. Along the way I read advice columns, personal ads, and newspaper accounts of affairs in many languages, and interviewed leading historians, psychologists, and sexologists. Wherever there was academic research on affairs, I combed through that, too.

And, of course, I interviewed scores of adulterers and their mates. To my amazement, although I was a stranger showing up with a voice recorder and a promise to change their names

(I did, along with some identifying details), people around the world told me their sexual secrets. By the time I left town, I was usually turning people away. Most interviewees expected to get something out of it. Britons, used to their competitive tabloid press, asked for cash payments (I refused). A psychologist in Moscow stretched our lunch to nearly three hours, long after he'd run out of things to say, so he could keep refilling his plate at an all-you-can-eat Uzbek buffet. Before we left, he pulled two crumpled bags from his pocket and stuffed them with cookies.

Many people spoke to me as favors to friends. Some foreign women wanted a girlfriend to confide in, and a Chinese man clearly hoped the interview was a date. A married banker in London, who'd been meeting women through the Internet, wanted to boast about his conquests to someone but didn't think even his close friends would understand. Several Frenchmen, who had never told anyone about their affairs, said they really just wanted to practice their English.

America was different. Nearly all the people I interviewed said they hoped that by telling their stories they'd help someone else. Americans of every walk of life and political persuasion said this—from a television producer in New Jersey to a computer salesman in Plano, Texas. A housewife in Atlanta couldn't understand that this book is neither self-help nor fiction. She wasn't sure what other kinds of books there are, and she wondered whether in any case I planned to include a list of useful phone numbers and Web sites. Outside of America no one said anything remotely like this. It didn't occur to them that talking about their affairs might be an act of public service.

People asked me a lot of questions, too, especially "Which country cheats the most?" and "Why did you choose this topic?" For the first question, I refer you to chapter 2. For the second—well, it's personal. I was intrigued by the rules of infidelity that I had glimpsed while living in different countries, and I wanted to understand America's own complicated, and often contradictory, ideas about cheating. And after nearly six years at the *Journal,* I aspired to write about something that had nothing to do with money (adultery turned out to be the wrong choice for this).

Once I focused on infidelity, it suddenly seemed to be the subject of every movie I saw and every novel I picked up. It struck me that if you take away extramarital sex, the canon of Western literature would be practically empty. Infidelity doesn't just weigh on American minds. All the people I spoke to, no matter which country they came from, had strong opinions about it. Everywhere I went, they pulled me into corners to describe their philandering bosses, friends, and parents. (Some of these stories are in the book.) I suddenly felt that, bubbling just below the placid, monogamous surface of daily life, there is another universe where lots of cheating goes on. The only person who didn't get excited about adultery was my ninety-year-old grandmother, who was raised in genteel South Carolina. When her friends asked her what I was writing about, she'd just say, "It's a book about love."

Differences between countries came out in the ways that people describe affairs. As in American slang, where we have someone "on the side," directional phrases are big in the rest of the world as well. Swedes and Russians both "sneak to the left," Israelis "eat on the side" (I'm told this is a particularly crude way of putting it), and Japanese "go off the path." The Irish "play offsides," a sporting term, while Englishmen "play away." For the Dutch, cheating is a journey in which the culprit "goes strange" or, more curiously, "pinches the cat in the dark." The destination is even vaguer for the French, who prefer *"aller voir ailleurs"*—literally "to go see elsewhere."

Some expressions downplay the seriousness of an affair. It's hard to get too upset about a "wonderful interval," the Indonesian expression for an affair that doesn't threaten either party's marriage. Japanese "sex friends" sound like singing cartoon characters. Not all euphemisms for cheating are so benign. During China's brutal Cultural Revolution in the 1970s, a person accused of having "lifestyle problems" could expect to lose his job and be publicly humiliated.

Other expressions are more literal. A philanderer in South Africa is a "running man," suggesting both the athleticism required for all his assignations and the fact that he's being pursued by his wife. (When caught, he might claim that the other woman was merely "passing here.") A Chinese man attempting to keep both his wife and his lover happy is trying to "stand in two boats at the same time," though if he's Taiwanese he might be excused as "a big white turnip with a colorful core." If your wife cheats on you in Tel Aviv, the neighbors might shrug and say, "A tied-up mare eats, too."

The most colorful expressions are reserved for the cheater's hapless spouse. Poles "make a balloon" out of their spouses, and a Chinese husband "wears a green hat." English and several other languages call the betrayed husband a "cuckold"— after the cuckoo bird who lays her eggs in other birds' nests. At least eight languages, including Romanian and Arabic, say the cuckold "wears horns." (In France you signal this by wiggling your index fingers on either side of your head.) This comes from the old custom of castrating a rooster and then—perhaps to signal that it's no longer virile—grafting the spike from the back of its leg onto its head, where it would grow into a horn. Go figure. Americans know the "horns" expression, but these days they prefer the moralistic "betrayed spouse," which leaves no doubt that there's both a crime and a victim.

The world is a big place. I went to countries where I had friends, knew the local language, or sensed I'd find good stories. I left out important countries. I apologize to the Indians and the Brazilians; I'm coming for you next. Although I spoke to experts and compared my observations with statistics, my own sample of adulterers isn't scientific. It's quirky, personal, and sometimes accidental. After several interviews fell through in Hong Kong, I was so desperate that I approached a man who was sitting with an attractive, much younger woman at a Starbucks. They weren't having an affair, but they were so intrigued by my project that they introduced me to their friends and acquaintances, some of whose stories appear in chapter 10.

This book doesn't ask whether we're genetically programmed to cheat or whether cheating has evolutionary benefits. I assume that people everywhere have roughly the same mix of biological urges. I want to know how people in different cultures channel those urges.

For my purposes, a cheater is someone who is supposed to be in a monogamous relationship but who's having secret sex with someone else. Blow jobs count. In fact, practically anything they don't want their partner to find out about—from a mere make-out session to a full-on romp—merits discussion. Cheaters needn't actually be married, particularly in European countries where marriage is increasingly unpopular but where people are still pairing up, having babies, and planning to be faithful. In America, where cohabitants cheat more and have lower status than married people, I sought out couples who had actually tied the knot. Stop reading here if you're hoping this is a book about swingers. Their sex is extramarital, but it isn't secret.

I don't get hung up on words like "cheating" and "unfaithful." Please don't either. In a book-length work on adultery, there are only so many ways to phrase it. After a few chapters, you'll be glad I didn't say "extradyadic pairings" or use the chaste Finnish expression "parallel relationships."

There's a form of hypochondria called "medical students' disease" in which students learning about an illness become convinced that they have it themselves. "The mere knowledge of the location of the appendix transforms the most harmless sensations in that region into symptoms of serious menace," one scientist explains.

Researching adultery is a bit like that. Spend all day reading about extramarital affairs and when your husband is an hour late from "soccer practice" or doesn't answer his cell phone on a "business trip," your mind lurches. Poor guy. Try proving you're not having an affair. It's much easier to rule out appendicitis.

My husband worried about me, too, perhaps with good reason. Hanging out with cheaters is a bit like hanging out with smokers; pretty soon you start itching for a cigarette. I did get some offers. But that blasted American guilt, which you'll hear a lot about, kept getting in the way.

welcome to america

THERE ARE A few things to know about April's affair. It ended nearly two years ago. It was the only time she was unfaithful during her twenty-year marriage. She changed departments at work and no longer supervises her former boyfriend. She claims it wasn't a love affair: it was a year and a half of raunchy e-mails (things like "I can't wait to see what's up your skirt") and clandestine meetings in parking lots and hotel rooms. It happened during a low point in her marriage, after April and her husband, Kevin, had lost most of their savings in the stock market and in a failed business venture. By the time Kevin found out about the affair, it was already over.

But two years later the subject of April's infidelity still dominates her marriage. Kevin, sixty-two, simply can't recover from it. He's convinced there were other affairs, too, and that April, forty-eight, might still be cheating.

It's hard to imagine when she'd have the chance. As punishment for her affair, Kevin has put April in a kind of suburban purdah. She leaves the house only for work or to go someplace with him. She no longer sees friends or invites her sister's kids for sleepovers. If she's a few minutes late coming home from work, Kevin leaves increasingly hostile messages on her cell phone. Even when she's home right on schedule, Kevin insists that she name everyone she spoke to that day. He searches her purse, checks her cell-phone bills, and randomly presses the re-dial button on their home phone to see who she's been calling. Several times she's discovered a voice-activated tape recorder in her car, meant to catch her if she calls someone on her way to or from work.

"I'm a whole different person than I used to be. I'm scared of talking to anybody. Kevin will say I'm fucking around," April says. She's gained 60 pounds since Kevin discovered her affair and her cholesterol is 277, well into the high-risk zone for heart disease. But when she wants to use the workout machines they keep in a spare room, she says Kevin becomes suspicious, saying, "You know the last time you lost weight . . ." Mostly she lies on the couch, her 210 pounds spread out around her.

When they're together, which is most of the time, Kevin and April have agonizing "cry talks" about the affair. Kevin has re-traced all the details of April's assignations with her lover. He learns more about affairs by reading self-help books and attending a weekly recovery group. "There should be total honesty in relationships, no secrets," he says. Recently he drove to

Nashville for a weekend seminar on affairs and came home convinced that infidelity runs in families and that—despite her denials—April's own parents must have cheated, too. The fact that April's affair was with a black man (Kevin and April are white) made it much worse for him.

I meet Kevin and April for lunch at a barbecue restaurant, near their home in a bedroom community just outside Memphis. Although half the residents of the surrounding county are black, their town is almost entirely white. Cars driving the tree-lined streets have bumper stickers like SCRAPBOOKER ON BOARD and MIRACLES HAPPEN. Residents earn more than twice as much as the average Tennessean. April has soft, freckled features and long, strawberry blond hair. Kevin is egg-shaped, with a round face and the voice of a radio announcer. Just a few minutes after I sit down, April is staring into her pulled-pork platter and weeping, while Kevin goes through the familiar catalog of her offenses.

Apparently I've hit them during a good period. "Neither of us cries as much as we used to, because of the antidepressants," Kevin says. They still flirt with divorce. But I get the impression that the affair has given their marriage, which was troubled before the affair, a reason for being. When they talk about certain episodes, it sounds like they're reminiscing.

"Remember the day I beat your picture to shreds?" Kevin says to April. "I went upstairs, I was sitting in the middle of the floor, I took a picture of her, and then I just started beating on it."

April's confused. Is Kevin talking about the time he shredded their wedding photos? Those are all gone, save for one that happened to be at Kevin's father's house.

No, Kevin means the time he beat a photograph of her with a recorder (the musical instrument) that happened to be within reach. "I just sat up there screaming my guts out. You know, 'I hate you, you miserable bitch, damn you,' and just screaming and yelling and beating it up."

It's the same spot, in the second-floor room where Kevin keeps his model airplanes, where he once sat for hours with his handgun to his head while April begged him to put it down.

April and Kevin might seem a bit extreme, but in many ways their experience is typically American. Two years of trauma after an infidelity is common. And, like many other Americans, April has trouble believing that she's now an "adulteress." She grew up in the church and thinks of herself as a "plain Jane." "I don't think it was me. I think it was almost like a different person," she says. "I've never thought of myself as being the type of person to have an affair."

SINCE THE 1970S, Americans have become more tolerant on practically every social issue to do with sex. We're more accepting of homosexuality, of unmarried people living together, of divorce, and of having sex and babies out of wedlock. Most Americans now have sex by the time they're seventeen but don't marry until they're about twenty-six, leaving a roughly nine-year stretch when they're sexually active but single.

So it's curious that on the topic of extramarital sex Americans have become stricter. In 1973, 70 percent of Americans said affairs were "always wrong." In 2001 roughly 80 percent said so, and most of the rest said affairs were "almost always wrong." In a Gallup Poll in 2006, Americans said that in moral terms, adultery was worse than both polygamy and human cloning.

Americans are divided on many topics, but on adultery we are strangely united. Kevin and April are Republicans who live in the Bible Belt. But when they talk about affairs they sound just like social progressives from New York City—perhaps plus the gun. Even Americans who don't practice any religion have a knee-jerk fervor about infidelity.

"I just don't think you can do it without feeling guilty. You're hurting everyone, including yourself," says one typical liberal, a thirty-two-year-old woman who works for a fashion designer in New York, lives in a downtown loft, and surrounds herself with like-minded friends. "You're dishonest, and when you're dishonest, it creates [more] dishonesty. No matter how clever you think you are, it eats away at you."

American adulterers regularly tell me, as April does, that they're not the sort of people who would cheat. It's hard to fault them for this small lapse of logic. Given how strongly Americans oppose extramarital sex, cheaters aren't just ordinary people who've erred; they're sinners removed from the rest of us. It's one thing to fall in love with a coworker; it's quite another to be labeled an infidel.

There are specific contexts—the occasional sports team or

law firm—where infidelity is tolerated or even encouraged. Liberals seem more likely to joke about cheating and to question whether monogamy works. But the stigma on infidelity is so powerful that it's hard to be blasé for long, especially when someone in your own life cheats.

At a bistro near his home on the Upper West Side of Manhattan, a businessman confesses to me that he's been faithful to his wife through more than twenty years of marriage. Having sex with someone else sounds appealing, but it also makes him visibly anxious. Among his circle of high-achieving friends, infidelity is so rare that "if it is there, it's an exception, it's an anomaly, it's a semi-crisis." There's the possibility of risking his double-income marriage and the equally fearsome problem of "What would my children think of me?"

The few people he knows who have affairs have lots of affairs. They flaunt their exaggerated sexual appetites, which in his view seem to run alongside glaring personality disorders. "You have to find people like that, people somehow out of the order of things. It's not about sex; it's about eccentricity or comedy," he says. Cheating also suggests an unseemly link to America's underclasses, who lack the resources or the discipline to create order in their lives. Joining either sort of company would be socially damaging. "I'm not sure I would want to be thought of as a person who has affairs. It does nothing for your status," he says.

Americans gain status by radiating an aura of monogamy. It signals that they're good parents, honest employees, or trust-

worthy merchants and that they share the values of other de-
cent folks. A doctor's wife in Miami tells me that, strictly speaking, she wouldn't mind if her husband had sex with someone
else. She'd be grateful to forego her weekly conjugal duties.
But she'd be devastated by what cheating would *say* about her
husband. She and all their friends know him as someone who's
steadfastly and happily monogamous. If he cheated, it would
seem as if he'd been fooling everyone and that they didn't really
know him.

American tales of adultery are usually couched in moralizing and end up—after a brief temptation—back in a monogamous safe zone. A woman named Betsy writing in *More,* a
leading magazine for women over forty, discovers that she has
a crush on her osteopath and immediately feels guilty for imagining what anyone besides her husband would look like naked.
Then she discovers that her girlfriends have crushes, too. A
photographer friend even had a onetime romp with her pool
boy. But the friend "regretted it. It went from being an adorable
little fantasy to something you've taken too far. You've lost control. Not that anyone found out, but I really, really shocked myself," the friend says.

Adultery is just too ethically outsize for Betsy even to fanta-
size about. When she imagines running away with the osteopath, "I sometimes placed the kids, both his and mine, in the
car, just to make sure they were safe." At her next appointment, each confesses the other is cute, but they quickly agree
that "all of this was in no way a good idea." She redeems the

whole unconsummated episode by saying it improved her mood and brought her out of a work slump. "You go back to your life safe, untainted, maybe a little guilty, but still a good person," she concludes.

Professional advice columns and online forums where people ask their peers for guidance draw from the same script. In one such forum, a divorcée says she's dating a wonderful man, but on a night out with girlfriends another man bought her a drink. "At the end of the night, when I was very drunk, I believe I kissed him. I think it was a peck. Not even sure. I barely remember it. And now I am devastated and sickened with what I have done. This is just not me, and I know I'll never ever, ever, do it again! Should I tell my boyfriend? How do I get over this? I feel like now I don't deserve him. Thank you so much for any advice you have to offer."

I MIGHT HAVE thought this was the natural way to look at infidelity, had I not known that educated, middle-class people in other countries handle affairs quite differently. Many consider our methods bizarre. They're baffled by our panicky confrontations, our knee-jerk threats of divorce, our faith in the redemptive power of marriage counseling, and even our assumption that honesty is the highest value of coupledom. They're especially amused by the Jekyll-and-Hyde performance that Americans have perfected in which an adulterer is reborn as an adultery guru who publishes his memoirs and

teaches others how to "survive" affairs. It's not just the after-
math of affairs that's different. Outside America, people have
their own ideas about whom to have an affair with, how obliged
the parties are to each other, and even how the whole thing
should end.

Infidelity may seem like a secret, lawless realm, in which
people make private decisions about how to behave. In fact,
even extramarital affairs have rules. We learn the rules through,
among other sources, stories and gossip about how affairs play
out. These shared narratives define what is "normal" in each
place and shape our expectations about what should happen to
a couple in the course of a long marriage. Of course, no one's
life follows the rules exactly. And some people deviate from
them on purpose. The point is that everyone in a society knows
what the rules are and where their own behavior stands in rela-
tion to the rules.

"When people tell me a little bit of their story, I don't need
to know the rest," says Peggy Vaughan, a Californian who runs
a telephone consulting service for people who've discovered
that their spouses are cheating. "I don't want to hear the blow-
by-blow, because whatever the specifics are, the emotional experience is so predictable. I could tell them what they're going
to say next."

We all know the American script. One part of it says a cheating husband is supposed to tell his mistress that he's unhappy
with his wife. This means he's not a lousy two-timer but rather
a sensitive soul who is understandably searching for the love

and affection he deserves. In China, however, I discover that married men routinely praise their wives to their mistresses, to prove they respect women and to set boundaries for the affair.

People everywhere may have the same menu of emotions. But cultural scripts teach us *which* emotions to invoke on a particular occasion. A married Japanese woman was confused when I asked her if she felt guilty about having a lover. I had to repeat the question several times. Feeling guilty hadn't occurred to her, since she was meeting her obligations to her family. A Frenchman was taken aback when I asked whether he had gone into therapy to sort out his double life. In fact, he had dropped out of therapy soon after meeting the woman who became his mistress, since he was finally happy.

There are some universals, of course. Even in countries where people supposedly tolerate cheating, almost everyone is heartbroken to discover an infidelity. But other details vary a lot. I always got a rise out of people outside America by telling them about "the talk," a dating rule in urban America that says a relationship isn't sexually monogamous until both parties explicitly say it is. Foreigners are astonished to learn that Americans keep up their online personal ads well into a courtship, until both parties decide to make the leap to monogamy. "Don't assume you're exclusive until you talk about it," warns a columnist on the dating Web site match.com. When you bring up the subject, "present your desire in an amiable way that shows you're open to a discussion about it."

Indeed, few other cultures even have American-style "dating," that period of comparison shopping when it's all right to juggle several budding relationships at once. In America the period of polyamorous courtship tends to last longer than it does elsewhere. And although people in other countries observe relationship milestones, they don't tend to discuss them explicitly. French philosopher Bernard-Henri Lévy writes that while he was standing in line at a Washington, D.C., airport, he overheard a young couple discussing whether they were still just dating or what the new parameters of their "relationship" were. He observes "this very un-French way of turning the date itself, and later the relationship as such, into a separate entity, living its own life alongside the two lovers."

Even after "the talk," quite a lot of cheating goes on among American daters (far more than in marriage). Each party assesses scores of candidates over the course of a decade and sometimes two. When at last a man and woman settle on each other and decide to marry, it's as if they've crossed the finish line. The rules of fidelity are different on the other side. Although we accept some cheating during the ruthless days of courtship, we expect übermonogamy from our new spouses. Women think, "'If he truly loved me, he couldn't even get an erection looking at another body, another breast.' If a man notices another woman in a restaurant, [his wife goes] nuts," says Diane Sollee, who runs a pro-marriage organization in Washington, D.C. "We've gotten so romantic in America. We think any violation of the romantic code is grounds for divorce."

With so much vigilance and guilt, how do married Americans ever manage to cheat? The answer is that there's more than one set of rules. The official rules say cheating is absolutely wrong. It's the kind of thing that people tell pollsters. But when people cheat, they're usually following another set of rules: the unofficial ones. In effect, as the sociologist James Farrer points out, each culture agrees on a shared set of stories about when it's okay to be unfaithful.

In America, a fulfilling marriage isn't just an ideal. It's seen as an entitlement. A hedge fund manager in New Jersey who was planning to leave his sweet but boring second wife to be with his girlfriend gave me his best puppy dog look and explained, "I need to be happy." The pursuit of happiness, or true love, is one of the most salient stories that Americans use to justify affairs and overcome their moral qualms about cheating.

Being unfaithful requires more than just the right set of stories. It also requires the opportunity to enact these stories. Are men and women allowed to be friends and thus spend time alone? Are husbands and wives expected to spend their leisure time together? Is it easy to get a baby-sitter? How large are homes? When I'm in Moscow, a family psychologist tells me that many Russians live in two-room apartments, with the parents and children in one room, and a set of grandparents in the other. "You can imagine how parents make love. . . . An affair for such a family may be a better choice than constantly fighting with the grandparents," he says.

Therapists in America describe a different problem—the fact that the discovery of an affair becomes the focus of a marriage for years on end. They say that this extended adultery seizure—during which everything else in life recedes into the background—is a typical phase.

There are people who never pull out of this phase. Twenty-five years ago, Neil got a phone call saying that his wife was in the hospital. She had been beaten up by her boss, in what appeared to be a lover's spat. Neil, then in his late thirties and vice president of a nonprofit organization in Baltimore, had suspected that something was going on between them. Finding out for sure sent him spiraling into what he describes as a "catatonic state" that he says he hasn't really come out of.

I meet Neil, now sixty-four, in the lobby of a suburban church in Memphis. He's a tall, elegant man with a square jawline. He likes basketball and playing with his grandchildren. But as he tells me the details of the affair, his dignity falters and his patrician features crumble. It's like watching Ward Cleaver come undone.

"There isn't a day—listen to me—there isn't a day that goes by where I don't think about this many times. I'm not talking about I think about it once in a fleeting moment and then I become engrossed in something else. No. It's just like this little pain in the back that keeps coming on you. It never goes away."

Neil can't believe that the pain of his wife's affair has lasted this long. He's an intelligent man. He's let go of plenty of other hurts and slights in his life. I find it strange, too. Of course a partner's infidelity would be distressing, insulting, and scary. But as I spoke to people across America, they kept trying to convey that, like Neil, they weren't just sad and wounded.

Their whole view of the world had collapsed. "It robs you of your past," one "betrayed spouse" explains. "What is real? What is fake?"

The American Association for Marriage and Family Therapy warns, "The reactions of the betrayed spouse resemble the post-traumatic stress symptoms of the victims of catastrophic events." People trying to describe this emotional free fall reach for the most extreme metaphor they can imagine. A woman in her forties who lives near Seattle says that "9/11 always reminds me of how it felt—one floor collapsing into another." Another, writing on a Web site for people with unfaithful spouses, compares the discovery of her husband's affair to the Asian tsunami of 2004, which killed a quarter of a million people.

"Many women feel so out of control they believe they are going crazy," Jo Ann Lederman, a couples therapist in Miami, writes in her advice column. "You can expect physiological changes in your nervous system and in your cognitive abilities." Lederman says a patient told her, "It felt worse than when our child died. Then, I knew doctors had done all they could. I never dreamed my husband, my best friend, would become the instrument of my torment and my grief."

MONOGAMY IS IN America's DNA. The Puritans who founded the American colonies in the seventeenth century famously punished adulterers with, at various points, public whippings and occasionally death. They really did order some convicted adulterers to affix the letter *A* (or sometimes *AD*) to "the outside of their uppermost garment," although, unlike Hester Prynne's judges in Nathaniel Hawthorne's novel *The Scarlet Letter,* they normally didn't specify the color. The Puritans used the biblical definition of adultery, which includes only a married or betrothed woman and her lover. Straying husbands were charged with the lesser crime of "fornication" (sex between people who aren't married).

As tensions grew between Britain and the American colonists in the eighteenth century, Britain justified its rule by saying that the two populations were like a parent and child. That analogy was an anathema to the colonists, who said they preferred a voluntary relationship with England, like that of a husband and wife.

When America became independent, its leaders again adopted marriage as a metaphor for how the new republic should govern itself. The Harvard historian Nancy Cott describes this brilliantly in her book *Public Vows: A History of Marriage and the Nation.* She says that for America's founders marriage symbolized political liberty. In both, each party voluntarily takes on obligations to the other, and each benefits from the relationship. Of course, the founders didn't have just any type of marriage in mind. For them the only proper marriage was the Christian model of one husband and one wife, sexually faithful to each other until the bitter end.

Marriage wasn't merely a metaphor. The founders also believed that married people make the best citizens. The behavior of individuals hadn't mattered much during the colonial period, because the British monarchs did what they wanted. In the new representative democracy, however, the choices of America's citizens would shape the character of the state. The strength and perhaps the very survival of their country hinged on the moral fitness of its citizens. The theory went that if the people were rotten and corrupt, they'd elect leaders who were, too.

The founders encouraged marriage in hopes of creating an orderly society that would put Americans on their best behavior. They imagined that wives would tame their husbands' unruly impulses, while husbands used their superior judgment to help their wives behave rationally. Political philosophers of the day wrote that marriage would encourage people to work selflessly for the public good. The idea filtered to popular magazines, which sang the benefits of loving, faithful relationships. The president's own family emerged as the archetype of the American household.

Early lawmakers didn't leave things to chance. If Americans didn't want to marry, they'd have to forgo sex. State governments, which controlled marriage laws, banned practically every kind of sex outside of marriage, including fornication, sodomy, and adultery. Offenses like "criminal conversation" (having sex with someone else's spouse), "enticement" (convincing a woman to leave her husband), and "alienation of affections" (taking affection from its rightful owner, the spouse) were punished with fines. These were crimes against a husband, since in legal terms his wife's body belonged to him. In case nonmarital sex was still tempting, in the nineteenth century most states banned abortion and the federal government made it illegal to mail "immoral" materials, which were assumed to include information on birth control, Cott writes.

By the start of the twentieth century, many Americans were tired of Victorian prudishness. Birth control was becoming widely available anyway, women all over the Western world were agitating for the vote, and Freud was arguing that people are motivated by their sex drives. Women, who were no longer assumed to be frigid, started believing that marital happiness included having satisfying sex.

Courts, as defenders of the national interest, were wary of these permissive attitudes. Some states upped adultery to a criminal offense punishable by as many as five years in prison and became more zealous in prosecuting civil laws against it. But they couldn't buck the social trend. Women got the vote in 1920, and most of the laws that made a wife her husband's property were stricken.

As the century wore on, the government loosened its hold on Americans' private lives. The U.S. Food and Drug Administration approved sales of the birth control pill in 1960. The Supreme Court struck down state bans on abortion in 1973. And in perhaps the most crucial step, from 1969 through the mid-1980s every state adopted some version of no-fault divorce. This meant that people could walk away from their marriages simply because they weren't happy. More and more women had their own paychecks and could ditch their husbands for offenses like adultery, which previous generations may have let pass. The national divorce rate shot up from 2.6

per thousand people in 1967 to 5.3 per thousand in 1979 (it has since fallen). Decisions about when and whether to have children and whether to stay in a marriage were left to individuals, with much less interference from the state.

As individuals got more control over procreation and marriage, adultery also assumed a new symbolic value. Instead of something that determines the fate of the nation, extramarital sex emerged as something that affects one's own family and personal life. Americans didn't stop caring about infidelity. On the contrary, they became stricter about it. And they continued imagining it as a gateway crime that could unleash all kinds of other ills. But, in the new view, these ills wouldn't be unleashed on the body politic; they'd be unleashed on the adulterer's own family and personal life. In effect, adultery was privatized. Most state adultery laws had been taken off the books, and those that remained were mainly cultural relics.

The idea that cheating on your spouse creates a slippery slope into personal chaos has become a standard plotline in Hollywood movies. When a main character in a drama cheats, the rule of thumb is that someone must die (not necessarily the cheater) as cosmic penance for the affair and as evidence of the evils that infidelity unleashes. One example is 2002's *Unfaithful,* a substantially rewritten remake of a French film, in which a suburban housewife falls into a steamy affair with a man she meets by chance on the street (since she's the heroine, she wasn't looking to cheat). In one scene, inserted for the benefit of American audiences, the woman's friends appraise the sexy Frenchman at the bar, not realizing the heroine is sleeping with him. One of the friends says she'd be "on her back in seconds" if the man were interested and that sleeping with him would be something she did for her own amusement, like taking a pottery class.

But the other friend warns that affairs are never that simple. "No, it would start out like that. And then something would happen, and someone finds out, or someone falls in love, and it ends disastrously. They always end disastrously."

Before long, the heroine's husband, who has been a model businessman and dad, discovers the affair and kills the Frenchman. Husband and wife reconcile, but it's clear they'll forever fear being implicated in the murder, or perhaps they'll succumb to the urge to confess. In any case, the affair has forever ruined their comfortable, quiet life.

I hear the same message in Internet chat rooms. When a woman writes that she might sleep with a married man to whom she is already emotionally bonded, a barrage of respondents— some of whom have had affairs themselves—warn that submitting to this short-term pleasure will ruin her life.

"Are you truly ready for the dual life this will require of you? Have you thought this out completely? Try to see yourself in life say in 1 year, 2 years, 5 years, 10 years into your future. An A[ffair] does and will affect the REST of YOUR life. Justifications aside, you still have to live with yourself. . . . This is not a situation I would recommend even to my worst enemy." Another writes, "I strongly urge you to break off all contact with this person and save yourself and your family months or years of hell on earth for all concerned."

In 1998, America staged its adultery script in perhaps the most public forum ever: the impeachment trial of President Bill Clinton. Clinton's Republican antagonists were careful to say they weren't trying Clinton for his extramarital trysts with Monica Lewinsky, the twenty-two-year-old intern at the White House. His real crime, though, happened to be the other moral violation most closely linked to extramarital sex in America: lying. To prove this charge, investigators created the 445-page "Starr Report" which described ten sexual encounters between Clinton and Lewinsky, starting from the time he first chatted her up during the shutdown of the government in November 1995 through to their meetings in the "windowless hallway outside the study" of the Oval Office.

The characters and the plotline of the "Starr Report" are straight from the standard American adultery script. Lewinsky is the mistress who aspires to supplant the wife, and Clinton is the husband who feeds her expectations in order to keep the sexual favors coming. According to the report, "President Clinton once confided in Ms. Lewinsky that he was uncertain whether he would remain married after he left the White House. He said in essence, '[W]ho knows what will happen four years from now when I am out of office?'"

The Starr Report lays out the familiar mistress's laments. One friend of Lewinsky's said that, "If [Lewinsky] was going to lie to me, she would have said to me, 'Oh, he calls me all the time. He does wonderful things. He can't wait to see me.' . . . [S]he would have embellished the story. You know, she wouldn't be telling me, 'He told me he'd call me, I waited home all weekend, and I didn't do anything, and he didn't call, and then he didn't call for two weeks.'"

Clinton's friend Vernon Jordan, a Washington lawyer, testified that when Lewinsky complained that Clinton didn't call or see her enough, "he felt the need to remind Ms. Lewinsky that the President is the 'leader of the free world' and has competing obligations." When Clinton's interest in Lewinsky wanes, she switches to another familiar role: that of the mistress using veiled threats of disclosure to walk away from the affair with at least some material benefits. In this case she wanted a job in New York.

Even Clinton's Democratic defenders were careful to establish their ethical bona fides. Senator Robert Byrd of West Virginia, an elder statesman of the party, called Clinton's behavior a "sorrowful spectacle." One of Clinton's own lawyers told the House Judiciary Committee that the president's affair with Lewinsky was "morally reprehensible." The only thing that was glaringly off script, which jarred Americans, was that Clinton's wife, Hillary, didn't leave him. Diane Sollee, the marriage expert in Washington, says that during the hearings journalists called her and demanded to know how the Clintons' marriage could possibly survive.

Clinton's Republican antagonists seemed not to have gotten the memo that adultery had become a private matter. They urged the nation to look at infidelity the old way, as something that threatened the stability of the nation. Several congressmen faced the television cameras with letters from schoolchildren who had been "heartbroken" when they learned that the president had deceived them. "If the president breaks the covenant of trust he's made with the American people, he can no longer be trusted. And because the executive plays so large a role in representing our country to the world, America can no longer be trusted," said Henry Hyde, the Republican congressman from Illinois who was the lead house manager during the impeachment trial.

But when it came to his own life, Hyde remembered that infidelity had become a private matter. After Salon.com disclosed in 1998 that Hyde had carried on a five-year affair in the late 1960s with a young mother called Cherie Snodgrass, Hyde—who was married himself, with four children at the time of the affair—issued a statement saying that "the statute of limitations has long since passed on my youthful indiscretions. Suffice it to say Cherie Snodgrass and I were good friends a long, long time ago." Hyde was forty-one when he began the affair.

Most Americans stuck to the idea that affairs are a private sin. Right after the House of Representatives voted to impeach Clinton, his national approval rating jumped ten points, to 73 percent, its highest level ever, according to a CNN/Gallup Poll. Meanwhile, approval for the Republican Party plunged twelve points, to 31 percent.

Clinton wisely used this more modern script as a guide for expiating the sin of extramarital sex. He might as well have been following the steps laid out by the American Association for Marriage and Family Therapy. Perhaps he was. An essay on the association's Web site explains that "to restore trust, the person who had the affair will need to be fully truthful and honest about any details that the injured spouse wants to know, such as the name of the other person involved in the affair and details of secret meetings and sexual encounters." After that, the adulterer should "assume full personal responsibility for the affair and not pass the blame onto the spouse, personal or emotional problems, or work pressures."

Clinton followed this practically to the letter. First he came out of denial and admitted to the affair. Then, just before the Starr Report was released, he went on tour to apologize to his supporters. "I have no one to blame but myself for my self-inflicted wounds," he said in a speech in Orlando, Florida. Democrats in Congress convened for a meeting with Clinton soon after his confession, where they apparently achieved an emotional catharsis. "I saw a profoundly distressed human being, angry at himself, evidencing to all of us a very deep regret, shame and anger at himself," one congressman told reporters afterward. "I saw real sadness about what he has done to his family." Ironically, the detailed disclosures in the Starr Report may have helped Americans make peace with their president.

THERE'S NO empirical evidence that people who are sexually faithful make better doctors, business partners, citizens, or presidents. Likewise, there's no proof that people who have extramarital sex embezzle money more often, commit more murders, tell more lies, or are generally more corrupt than those who are faithful. As far as I know, no one's found a correlation between a company's stock price and who its CEO is sleeping

with. The belief that cheating on your spouse is part of a con-
stellation of character flaws and misbehaviors may be true, but
it hasn't been tested. For every bad president who had a mistress, there's a good one who did, too, or another bad one
who didn't.

Because of the frenzied way that Americans tend to handle
adultery, however, an infidelity does seem to make life a lot
more chaotic. A few months after I first meet Kevin and April,
I phone them to see how they're doing. April happens to be
home alone. She says the situation is quite bad. In fact, her life
has become engulfed in the kind of chaos that movies warn
about. On one of his routine searches of April's purse, Kevin
found a printout of an e-mail she'd received from John, her former lover. John wrote that he was having problems at home
and wondered if he and April could talk. April says she left the
e-mail in her purse because she didn't think she had anything
to hide.

I'm not sure whether this was a misjudgment or a deliberate
provocation. In any case, according to April, when Kevin read
the e-mail, he got out his gun and said he was going to John's
house. There were some racial epithets. In the course of leaving
the house, Kevin grabbed April so hard he bruised her arm. He
got as far as the garage when April called the police. They arrived and arrested him, and Kevin spent several hours in jail.

April and Kevin have already paid fifteen hundred dollars in
legal fees, and Kevin's lawyer has asked for e-mails and anything else documenting April's affair, to build Kevin's court
case. The process will probably drag out for months. April says

that when Kevin is home, he sits around and says he doesn't know if he'll ever be happy again. "The last couple of weeks, I'm finally starting to realize this isn't all my fault," she says.

April's so upset about what's happened, and about the fact that her affair is still consuming their lives, that she lets something slip: Her relationship with Kevin began as an affair. Kevin had told me he and April worked together but that they began dating only after he divorced his second wife. Kevin, it seems, lies about sex, too.

"He kept promising he would get a divorce," April says. "That went on for about— We had an affair for probably three years." Kevin's wife and her mother once showed up on April's doorstep "banging on my door and calling me a damn husband stealer." According to April, Kevin cheated on his first wife as well.

Pointing out the similarities in their behavior hasn't brought April any relief from Kevin's obsession with her affair. "He says the one where he was having affair with me was different because he was in love with me. I say, 'Yeah, but we weren't in love at the beginning,'" April says. "He says he's learned from the way I treated him, and now he feels bad for what he put them through."

lies, damn lies, and adultery

When I started researching this book, I figured I'd include a master ranking of countries from the most to the least adulterous. I didn't know if such a list already existed or whether I'd have to draw it up myself. It was hard to imagine how it would look. Where would America rank? Which nation would have the dubious distinction of topping the list? Would there really be big differences between countries? Would the rankings correlate to something weird, like the weather?

My first inkling that the world doesn't offer up its sexual secrets so easily comes in Moscow, when I visit the man who's considered the father of Russian sexology. In person, Igor Kon, seventy-six, looks more like its grandfather or maybe its mascot. He's just over five feet tall, with a full head of white hair, a cuddly smile, and the endearing habit of mixing academic jargon with words like "masturbation" and "erection." He's so prolific he's not even sure how many books he's written but says it's "about fifty." Kon's peers at the World Association of Sexual Health recently awarded him their gold medal for lifetime achievement.

Every surface of Kon's home office is crammed with books, papers, and journals written in a half dozen languages. I figure somewhere among these piles are the results of national sex surveys with statistics for infidelity in Russia and probably many other countries. I envision the Yoda-like Kon taking out that master list I've been fantasizing about and creaking, "Slovenia you will go to, and Niger next." Maybe he'll offer a tantalizing glance and then put it away.

But when I mention Russian sex statistics, Kon's tone turns from cheerful to glum. "There were never and will not be in the foreseeable future national surveys," he tells me. Kon says governments are the natural choice for funding expensive national surveys, which typically include a few questions about extramarital sex. But Soviet governments barely permitted any public discussion of sex, let alone a survey that might embarrass the state by showing that Russians were engaging in banned activities like extramarital affairs.

Though the Soviet Union collapsed in 1991, Kon says Russia's Orthodox Christians now keep the current government from funding practically anything related to sex. A national survey would be a treasure trove for Kon and his colleagues. Instead they have to work with the limited data they gather themselves, the best of which is a 1996 survey of St. Petersburg.

Sex research in Russia has few perks. Kon earns the equivalent of $123 a month as a chief researcher at the Russian Academy of Sciences. That's scarcely enough to buy food in Moscow. He and other sex researchers work several jobs just to scrape by. And researching sex is hazardous. Vandals defaced the door to Kon's apartment. He shows me a seventy-four-page pamphlet in which a group of Russian academics denounced him as a "danger to the Russian society and state" and accused him of supporting pedophilia (he doesn't). While he was delivering a lecture at Moscow University in 2001, a gang of about twenty hoodlums held up signs "accusing" him of being gay and then threw a cream pie in his face. At least Kon didn't have to worry about the people who called and threatened to bomb his home. If they were serious, they would have done it without warning. "To kill someone in Moscow is not a big problem. If they wanted to kill me, it was very easy to do."

RESEARCHING SEX ANYWHERE is not for the faint of heart. Moments into my interview with Alain Giami, the director of research at the French National Institute of Health and Medical Research, he cuts me off midsentence and becomes so agitated I'm afraid he's going to leap over his desk.

My offense is that I used the word "infidelity."

"What do you call 'infidelity'? I don't know what 'infidelity' is," he rants. "I don't share this view of things, so I would not use this word. It implies religious values. By using 'infidelity' it's a negative value. It means you're not faithful, you're a liar."

I have entered the war of words over what social scientists should call affairs. When they write about the topic in professional journals and academic publications, they try to sound morally neutral. But Giami isn't even comfortable with language implying that the interviewee is married or heterosexual or that the affair is less important than the main relationship. He insists on a phrasing that, to me, sounds more suited to accounting than sex. "We call them simultaneous multipartnerships," he says.

Academics seem to delight in coming up with spiffy new names. If I ever cheat, I plan on telling my husband I was merely "sexually networking," the phrase researchers in Nigeria use (mistresses were SGFs, for "steady girlfriends"). In the 1980s, American academics tried to coin the acronym EMC for "extramarital coitis," but this didn't catch on, perhaps because it sounds like a medical procedure. No academics say "adultery," which seems to be preceded by an imaginary voice from above intoning, "Thou shalt not commit."

What all these expressions refer to is another issue. Some surveys just ask about "sex" with someone other than a partner and let respondents decide what this means. Others try to phrase it as a positive question, such as, "Were you monogamous in the last year?" In some cases I wish the questions were a bit more vague. I blush at the thought of an American "random-digit dialing" phone survey done in 1990 in which the caller demands to know, "Over the past twelve months, how many different people have you had either vaginal or anal intercourse with?"

Other questions try to conjure a mood. An American survey done in 1992 defined sex as a "mutually voluntary activity with another person that involves genital contact and sexual excitement or arousal, that is, feeling really turned on, even if intercourse or orgasm did not occur." Just reading that feels a bit like cheating.

Some surveys are clearly done for entertainment and don't bother concealing their biases. A poll in one South African magazine has separate categories for men who cheat and men who cheat "while drunk." One French polling firm measured "Infidelity of Women on Vacation." Respondents were supposed to choose their favorite from among three types of potential lovers (the runaway favorite was a "super-funny man, even if he isn't handsome or intelligent"). Almost as an afterthought, there was a fourth box for women who said they wouldn't cheat.

China's Health and Family Life Survey, done in 2000, asked, "Nowadays in our society, some married people have sex with those other than their spouse (extramarital affair, third party). Do you think that each such case should be treated individually or that these people should all be punished?"

In a country like China, where research on sex began only in the 1980s, the whole idea of sitting down with a stranger and revealing details of your sex life is unnerving. In the mid-1990s, a Chinese academic who reviewed the previous decade of research concluded that Chinese respondents typically believe female interviewers are "bad women" and that an interviewer who asks about a certain sexual practice does so because he fancies it himself. He also found that when questioned about sexual matters, "most females feel like vomiting."

These issues don't bode well for my adultery chart. How can I compare surveys on infidelity from different countries if they don't measure the same thing? Some surveys ask if a person has cheated during any marriages or even during any cohabiting relationships over his or her lifetime. Others ask only about the twelve months prior to the survey, figuring people have much better recall of a shorter period. Polls that specify that they're interested only in intercourse potentially exclude the thousands of people who've exchanged oral sex or merely had passionate make-out sessions in office parking lots. Don't those people count, too?

Researchers do what they can to induce their subjects to tell the truth. They'll ask the same question several different ways at different points in the interview and then see if the answers are consistent. Some put the most sensitive questions on a laptop computer and let the interviewee fill out the answers, so she doesn't have to "confess" to the questioner. In one study in the mid-1990s, interviewers asked a respondent's spouse to fetch them a glass of water so they could quickly ask a series of questions about sex without the significant other in earshot.

In the survey done in 2000 in China, researchers got their subjects out of the house, but their alternative arrangement sounds curiously like a seduction: "As a rule we invited each respondent to come to our room in a hotel as prearranged and meet an interviewer of the same sex in a closed room setting, talking one to one, while the interviewer tried his/her best to persuade the interviewee to provide honest answers." In America in the 1990s, researchers from the University of Chicago prescreened their subjects and discovered that Americans of all genders and races are most comfortable discussing sex with middle-aged white women. So they hired a platoon of such women and trained them not to flinch when respondents used "vernacular language" or described details of their sexual experiences.

Of course, even perfectly crafted polls are meaningless if pollsters don't select people to interview in the right way. It's Statistics 101: Everyone in the population you're trying to generalize about should have an equal chance—or at least a known chance—of being selected. This method, called probability sampling, is done by getting lists of the whole population and randomly choosing people to interview, or choosing them randomly from within certain categories like age or gender. If you stand on a street in Paris and interview pedestrians at random, your results won't necessarily reveal anything about all Parisians. People who frequent that street have a greater chance of being interviewed than everyone else in the city does, and they might have different tastes and habits than people in other neighborhoods. A probability sample, in which people are selected at random from a list of all Parisians, would be representative of the city because all residents had an equal chance of being questioned.

Ditto if the subjects of the study can volunteer to be interviewed. An example of this is the Global Sex Survey 2005, conducted by the British condom maker Durex. Durex used this survey to produce the kind of infidelity master list I've dreamed about. The company ranks levels of extramarital sex among people of forty-one countries, from Turkey (where 58 percent of respondents claim to have cheated) all the way down to Israel, with just 7 percent.

Durex officials say they surveyed 317,000 people. But all of these people were volunteers who clicked on the company's Web site and filled out its online survey. A few eager Turks could have entered hundreds of times. The only thing the survey might reliably suggest is that many respondents were teenagers, since in another section a third say they enjoy sneaking into their parents' bedrooms to have sex.

Academic work on affairs often has similar problems, since researchers can't get funding for large-scale studies. For her 1992 investigation of why people cheat, a respected American psychologist named Shirley Glass (mother of public radio host Ira Glass) resorted to handing out mail-in survey forms to white people at the Baltimore-Washington International Airport and then again during the lunchtime rush at a Baltimore office park. Her results may reveal something about those people, whoever they were, but they can't be used to generalize about anyone else. (The cheating women in her sample overwhelmingly justified their affairs by saying they had fallen in love with their affair partners, while most men said that "sexual excitement" justified their infidelities. No subsequent research has definitively shown why people cheat.)

I got very excited when I heard about the International Sexuality Description Project, which interviewed people in fifty-six countries. *Psychology Today* magazine quotes its findings on global "mate poaching" trends. But, as the directors of the study acknowledge, most of their respondents were hand-picked college students. And in many places so few people returned the surveys that the researchers had to group together all Africans and then all the South Americans.

When academics want to prove that it's important to study infidelity, they often cite a paper called "Causes of Conjugal Dissolution: A Cross-Cultural Study," in which anthropologist Laura Betzig finds that adultery is the leading cause of divorce in 186 cultures. When I finally have a look at this paper, however, it doesn't seem like the basis for claims about the way people in industrialized countries behave today. The cultures Betzig describes are mostly indigenous groups like the Bella Coola, the Yuroks, and the Pomos of North America, and she relies on accounts dating back to the nineteenth century.

ONE CONSOLATION in my quest for statistics is that I already know the American numbers: Half of men and a quarter of women have cheated on their spouses. When I start out, I'm not sure where these numbers come from, but I've heard them tossed around so many times that they seem like gospel.

As I begin digging through the scientific data on extramarital sex, these numbers crop up a lot. The source is Alfred Kinsey, the zoologist–turned–sex scientist from Indiana University who published his famous studies on American sexuality in 1948 and 1953. Kinsey's actual results are even racier than what's usually quoted: Fifty percent of men and 26 percent of women had had extramarital sex by age forty.

Americans were shocked when Kinsey published these numbers. Although it was hard to imagine that so many people were fooling around, the statistics were the first of their kind, so there was nothing to compare them to. They stuck in America's collective imagination and cemented the idea that infidelity is a national menace. As I found in my research, experts on infidelity still cite them.

So I was surprised to discover that Kinsey's numbers are extremely problematic. Though probability sampling was becoming the gold standard in the 1930s, sex research was a brand-new field, and Kinsey assumed that randomly chosen Americans wouldn't be willing to discuss their sex lives. Instead he and his team toured America and persuaded people they encountered to sit for case histories. Almost all of Kinsey's data comes from about eighteen thousand men and women who were mostly young and white. Kinsey tried to compensate for his "volunteer bias" by interviewing all the people he found in each setting. Still, he picked the setting. There's no reason to believe that his respondents represent all Americans, or indeed anyone but themselves. A member of the American Statistical Association's review team in the early 1950s told Kinsey, "I would trade all your eighteen thousand case histories for four hundred in a probability sample."

In the decades that followed, other unreliable surveys reinforced Kinsey's numbers or "discovered" even higher levels of infidelity. Magazines surveyed their readers and came out with outrageous numbers (*Cosmopolitan* magazine declared that 69 percent of married women over thirty-five had affairs). In the 1970s self-styled sexologists like Shere Hite sent out batches of surveys to women in political groups and put ads in women's magazines. Their results were titillating and got lots of press, but they were of dubious significance, too. Hite determined that 72 percent of men had cheated, and in a later poll she found that 70 percent of women married five years or more had cheated.

But these polls were all anyone had to go on. When scientists identified the virus that causes AIDS in 1984, they had to use Kinsey's numbers to assess the virus's likely path through the population, via high-risk behaviors like infidelity and anal sex, Julia Ericksen says in her book *Kiss and Tell.*

Researchers needed some new data, but U.S. officials seemed as reluctant as the Soviets to discuss sex. When a U.S. government institute requested proposals to design a national sex survey in 1987, the project was assigned the euphemistic name Social and Behavioral Aspects of Fertility Related Behavior. The word "sex" wasn't mentioned anywhere in the request for proposals. A group based at the University of Chicago's National Opinion Research Center won the contract. But conservative Republicans in Congress, who had to approve the study's funding, soon tried to block it. Senator Jesse Helms of North Carolina and others described the survey as a plot to legitimize gay relationships, pressed researchers to eliminate questions on masturbation, and insisted that they cease questioning anyone who claimed to be monogamous. These concessions weren't enough. In 1992, funding for the survey was blocked.

JUST AS I'm starting to despair about creating my adultery rankings, I hear about Finland. In sexology circles, Finland is known for having Europe's best sex research. The Swedes were the first to do a national sex survey using probability sampling, in 1967, but the Finns followed them in 1970 and have been monitoring their citizens' ejaculations, erectile dysfunctions, and extramarital affairs ever since.

They're innovators in the field. For the 1970 study, Finnish researchers sent uniformed nurses door-to-door to do the questioning and got a 91 percent response rate. "When a nurse comes to ring your doorbell, you don't throw her out so easily," says Osmo Kontula, who directed Finland's national surveys in 1992 and 1999.

There's a lot of sex to study. In the 1999 poll, 41 percent of Finnish men and a third of women said they'd had a "parallel relationship" during their lifetimes. In 1992 the men's proportion was 52 percent, while the women's was 29 percent. Although I still don't have a sense of the global landscape, this strikes me as quite a lot of cheating.

Kontula says Finns aren't ambivalent about sex. They see it as a positive experience. He says that unlike their counterparts elsewhere in Scandinavia, Finnish media don't focus on the perils of sex, such as diseases and unwanted pregnancies. Also, Finns travel a lot, creating opportunities for affairs. I am struck by the sexual biographies taken by Kontula and his colleagues. Many Finns they profile don't assume, as Americans often do, that sex inevitably wanes over the course of a long relationship. Many Finns think it will improve over time.

Kontula, who's now with the Population Research Institute in Helsinki, tells me, "Of course people are prone to be faithful to their partners. But if there is a chance, and they feel that no one will get to know about this, this is a temptation that is not easy to resist. Because these experiences are considered positive and valuable, as such."

In one biography a married policeman with three children describes a night out with his colleagues: "After we had bathed in the sauna and sat socializing, we went off to check out the local bar scene. The music was playing and the liquor flowed. . . . At the bar I noticed I was sitting with a nurse who was obviously older than me and who I knew had just got divorced. I asked her to dance and was greedily pressing her against me. She wasn't very beautiful, my wife is more beautiful even, but something in her made my desire rise and I began to pester her to make me a pot of coffee. . . ."

There must be something about that cold corner of the world. I've also tracked down the 1996 study of St. Petersburg, which is a five-hour train journey from Helsinki. St. Petersburg doesn't represent all of Russia, but the results of the study suggest that national statistics for Russia could be formidable. Some 55 percent of men and 26 percent of women said they'd had "extra sexual relationships" during their current marriages.

Americans finally got around to doing some proper national research, too. In 1988, scientists at the National Opinion Research Center added a question about the number of sexual partners in the last year to the General Social Survey, a far-reaching survey of American households they'd been conducting every year or two since 1972. In 1991 they began asking whether respondents had ever had extramarital sex.

The results were tamer than anything Kinsey or subsequent researchers had imagined. In 1991 just 21 percent of American men and 10 percent of women said they had ever had sex with someone other than their spouses while married. These numbers increased in some subsequent polls, but they never came anywhere near Kinsey's numbers. In 2004, 21 percent of men and 12 percent of women—altogether just 16 percent of adult Americans—confessed to having strayed at least once. That could mean just once in the course of a forty-year marriage.

Asking married people whether they've had more than one sex partner in the last twelve months could mean including a period when those people weren't married. But I prefer this to the "lifetime" levels of infidelity because, over a sexual lifetime, memories fade and marriages come and go. I can imagine thinking that a dalliance that happened twenty years ago is better forgotten. A lover in the last year is easier to remember.

By this twelve-month measure, Americans look particularly

chaste. In 1991 just 5.4 percent of married men and 3.4 percent of married women said they'd had more than one partner in the last year. In 2004 the figures were 4 percent of married men and 3 percent of married women. It became clear that Americans aren't rampant adulterers with daring, secret sex lives. In fact, for the most part, we're as boringly monogamous as we appear.

There's no way to be sure if these figures accurately reflect the way Americans behave. But researchers were encouraged to find that infidelity figures in the General Social Survey matched almost exactly those in the National Health and Social Life Survey, a broad national sex survey published in 1994 by the University of Chicago team, which eventually found private funding.

Other social scientists soon began analyzing the raw data that these national surveys provided. For the first time, they had empirical research on who cheats and when they do it. One group of researchers determined that women are most prone to stray during their twenties and men while they're in their thirties. In midlife the genders diverge. A woman's likelihood of having had an affair in the last year was practically nil by the time she reached her fifties.

Men's percentages for the past year were steady at just over 3 percent during their forties and fifties, but they slowed when the men reached their sixties. However, just when you think older men are settling down for the long haul, they bounce back. About 3 percent of married men in their seventies said they'd had more than one partner in the last year. It seems like a classic case of opportunity: After age sixty-five there are about four women for every three men, and the gender gap widens the older you get.

These virile seniors of all colors don't hold a candle to African-Americans. Between 1988 and 2004, 7.4 percent of married blacks and 3.1 percent of married whites said they'd had more than one partner in the last year. In the 1994 survey, 12 percent of black men said they'd had extramarital sex in the last year, compared with 3 percent of white men. Among women, the percentages were 7 percent of blacks and just over 1 percent of whites.

There aren't good data on how often adultery leads to divorce. However, not surprisingly, the two are strongly linked. In the General Social Surveys done between 1991 and 2004, 10.5 percent of people who were married and 11 percent of widows and widowers said they'd ever had an affair. However, 31 percent of divorced people and 22 percent of those who had remarried said they'd ever cheated on a spouse. People who described themselves as currently "separated" were the most promiscuous: Forty percent said they'd had extramarital sex.

Location matters, too. According to the General Social Survey, residents of America's twelve biggest cities cheated more than anyone else between 1988 and 2004. About 6 percent of the big-city residents had cheated in the last year, compared with 3 percent of suburbanites and 2.6 percent of rural residents.

But it's not the urban elites who are doing most of the cheating. The new data showed that America's underclasses seem to commit a disproportionate amount of adultery. Those with household incomes below $10,000 were more than twice as likely to have cheated in the past year as those with incomes above $60,000. Likewise, people who hadn't finished high school had the highest twelve-month cheating rates (5.2 percent), followed by high school graduates (3.4 percent) and graduates of junior colleges (3.6 percent). Holders of bachelor's degrees (2.5 percent) and graduate degrees (3 percent) had been the most faithful in the previous year. However, lifetime rates of cheating were similar for people with nearly all levels of education.

The statistics that have gotten the most attention are the ones about women. There's something about cheating wives that appeals to magazine editors everywhere. I've seen versions of the "women are cheating more" feature in Japan, Russia, Brazil, and France, and no doubt it's appeared in other countries, too. An American version ran as *Newsweek*'s cover story on July 12, 2005, under the titillating headline "The Secret Lives of Wives." The story practically salutes the idea that wives are claiming territory once occupied by their husbands. *Newsweek* explains that women now have more opportunities to meet potential lovers in the workplace, and they're more willing to risk affairs because they have their own money to fall back on if their marriages implode. The writers quote women who are enjoying the kind of recreational flings—often with personal trainers and other hired help—that used to be the purview of men. They cite statistics from the new sex studies, showing that between 1991 and 2002, the share of women who said they'd ever been unfaithful rose from 10 percent to 15 percent. Over the same period, men's infidelity levels rose much more slowly, from roughly 21 percent to 22 percent. The male level has barely shifted since 1996.

When I look more closely at the American numbers, however, this "trend" seems flimsier. In the four national surveys conducted between 1991 and 1996, women and men under forty-five were already cheating at the same rates, according to an academic paper called "Understanding Infidelity: Correlates in a National Random Sample." In the 1992 American survey, women aged eighteen to twenty-nine reported more affairs than men in the same age group.

And after the *Newsweek* story came out, so did the figures for infidelity in 2004. They showed that women reported lower lifetime infidelity rates in 2004 (11.7 percent) than they did in 1993 (12.8 percent). And women's cheating levels for the last twelve months were practically the same in 2004 (3.1 percent) as they were in 1988 (2.8 percent). In other words, there is no proof that female infidelity has jumped since the early 1990s, or anytime before that. "There's enough year-to-year bounce in the figures that one can't say for sure that there's been an increase," says Tom W. Smith, director of the General Social Survey.

There's not even good circumstantial evidence that women are cheating more than they used to. I'd expect a big shift in women's behavior to be accompanied by a change in attitudes about affairs, as women try to justify cheating. But between 1991 and 2001, the period when women supposedly broke out of their monogamous straitjackets, Americans became even more disapproving of infidelity.

It's hard to know whether, as the *Newsweek* article asserts, working women have more opportunities to cheat. The big jump in the number of working women happened in the 1970s and 1980s. But the first reliable sex statistics appeared only in 1988, so we have no way of knowing if American women are more promiscuous today than they were in the 1970s. As you'll see in the next chapter, some women now in their seventies describe the 1960s and 1970s as adultery heydays, and they can't believe how prudish their children are. These women had plenty of time to cheat, because they didn't have to report to an office every day. Even in the 1991 American sex survey, cheating was most likely to happen in households where one partner went out to work and the other stayed home.

HUNTING DOWN STATISTICS on infidelity is a bit like chasing fireworks. Every time I find a promising paper, it doesn't quite have the right numbers, but its bibliography lists four or five other papers that look promising. So I hunt down those papers, too, paying a fortune in download fees or begging favors from my friend David at the New York Public Library, who e-mails them or posts them to me in Paris. These new papers don't have the statistics either, but again each has several promising references, and I chase those down, too.

This cycle has been going on for months when yet another envelope from David arrives. It contains a 1995 paper called "Sexual Behavior in Developing Countries: Implications for HIV Control." On the second page is a chart showing the number of "non-regular" sexual partners that men and women in eighteen countries had in the twelve months prior to the surveys. Most of the countries are in Africa, but Hong Kong, Thailand, Sri Lanka, and the city of Rio de Janeiro are also included. All use probability samples. And they ask similar questions in each country, making it easy to compare results.

The chart isn't a ranking of infidelity, because it includes people who live alone. But it suggests that there are scientists out there looking for roughly the same numbers I am and that my global adultery ranking might consist of more than three countries. I am so excited I start to panic. What if I lose the pages in front of me and can't remember the title? What if rain comes through the window and soaks them?

I quickly send an e-mail to one of the authors, a bigwig at the prestigious London School of Hygiene & Tropical Medicine. Would he happen to have any numbers for married or cohabiting people? He writes back to say I should speak to Martine, a colleague who's preparing a paper using more recent data. There's new data? I breathlessly write to Martine, who is extremely busy preparing her paper but might have those numbers if I'll just contact her in several weeks.

When I e-mail her on the appointed day, I try to sound casual:

Hi Martine,
I hope your writing has been going well—I can sympathize
with the hours you must be putting in. You suggested that
I bother you around now to see if you had decided to calcu-

late the share of MARRIED people who'd had more than one partner in the last year . . .

She refers me to her colleague Emma, who the very next day sends the following e-mail:

Hi Pamela,
I did calculate this—along with 101 other things! I've attached a spreadsheet showing the % of currently married or cohabiting men and women who reported more than one sexual partner in the year before the survey. . . .

I can practically hear angels singing as I open the attachment. There are thirty-six countries, from Armenia to Zimbabwe, with the rates of infidelity for both men and women. Add these numbers to the dribs and drabs of statistics I've found elsewhere and it looks like I have the makings of a global ranking of cheaters. It's not comprehensive. Japan, India, and indeed most of Asia and the Middle East aren't on it, and not all the data are exactly comparable. Emma warns me that the levels in some places are high because they include polygamists and that, in later surveys, interviewers may have rushed respondents through repeated questions on infidelity. But given all the obstacles in sex research, it's not a bad start.

The numbers from Emma reveal astonishing levels of infidelity in poor countries. In Nigeria, 15 percent of cohabiting or married men say they had more than one partner in the last twelve months. In Haiti, it's 25 percent of men. In both the

Ivory Coast and Cameroon, it's 36 percent of men. Togo, a west African nation that's roughly the size of West Virginia, tops the list at 37 percent.

Latin lovers live up to their reputations. The twelve-month percentages for men were 8.6 percent for Bolivians, 12 percent for Brazilians, and 13.5 percent for Peruvians. A separate 2001 survey of men in Mexico City puts the figure there at 15 percent. I keep reminding myself that these are just the men who strayed in the last year. I can only imagine the lifetime rates. If 29 percent of men in Mozambique cheated in the last year, how many will stray in the course of a lifetime? All of them?

Then there's the other end of the chart, with Australians, Americans, and most Europeans. To my surprise, America sits squarely in the middle of this section. Although Italian men have a reputation for being advanced philanderers, according to these numbers Italians (3.5 percent annually) cheat less than Americans (4 percent). Men in Switzerland (3 percent) and Australia (2.5 percent) hover near the bottom.

Women are another matter. According to this list, while the poor men of the world are out gallivanting with their girl-friends and lovers, their partners are sitting chastely at home. All around the world, the biggest "risk factor" for infidelity is simply being male. But the difference between men and women is much greater in poor countries. In the same years that about 20 percent of men were unfaithful in Burkina Faso and the Dominican Republic, less than 1 percent of women in each of those countries said they cheated. There are only a handful of countries where more than 2 percent of women say they had more than one partner in the last year. Women in Nepal, the Philippines, and Mali appear to be almost magically monogamous: Zero percent report having had two or more partners in the previous year.

By contrast, women in rich countries tend to cheat more than women in poor countries, though sometimes not by a very large margin.

THIS PROBLEM HAUNTS sex researchers everywhere. How can women report lower rates of infidelity than men? Are married men just bedding single women? Or out-of-towners? Or is there, as some researchers investigated in the 1990s, a mythical group of women—possibly prostitutes, possibly just freelance mistresses—who are running around servicing lots of married men?

Another possibility is that respondents suffer from what social scientists call a "self-presentation bias." That is, they lie. Men inflate their conquests, and women underreport them, as both play to gender stereotypes. Lots of studies have been done showing that, even in anonymous polls, respondents strive to give "correct" answers, even if they aren't true.

Or maybe not everyone lies but a few people lie a lot. An academic in Britain found that if you strip away the men who claim to have had twenty or more sexual partners in their lifetimes, the ratio between the male and female numbers becomes almost even. He suggests dropping these outliers to get the real numbers.

It's actually true that infidelity tends to correlate with the weather. Generally speaking, people in warm places are more promiscuous. (Scandinavia and St. Petersburg are exceptions.) But, for the most part, the statistics lay out a world divided between wealthy countries where men and women cheat relatively little and poor countries where the percentage of men who cheat is in the double digits. Money is the international dateline for adultery. On one side you cheat. Cross to the other and you don't.

There are some exceptions. Kazakhstan, which is almost half Muslim and has an annual per capita income of $8,200, is the most faithful country I've found. Nepal, with an average income of $1,400, isn't far behind. Men from a few other poor countries, including Rwanda, the Philippines, and Bangladesh, appear to be pretty faithful, too. On the other hand, Norwegian men inch into the double digits.

My observation is that even rich people who live in poor countries cheat as much as, or more than, everyone else who lives there. In Brazil researchers canceled out the effects of income and found that how much men cheated depended on whether they lived in the north or the south. It turns out that countries, regions, and even neighborhoods have their own sexual cultures, which influence whether people are monogamous or not.

Americans disapprove of affairs more than people in most other countries do. But when it comes to behavior, we have about the same percentage of affairs—per capita, if you will—

as people in other industrialized countries. At the same time, we imagine ourselves as a nation of rampant cheaters, when in fact, if the statistics are to be trusted, marital infidelity is a fairly rare occurrence. Only 16 percent of American adults say they've had an affair in their lifetimes. In a given year, just 3.5 percent of adults will commit adultery. And it's been at roughly this level since Americans started keeping records in 1988. Adultery isn't an epidemic in America. It's the practice of a small share of the population, some of the time.

So why is it that in some circles quite a lot of cheating goes on? That's because America, like any country, doesn't have only one sexual culture. It has many. People don't just look to national television shows and presidents for guidance about whether to cheat on their partners. They look to their family, neighbors, and friends.

INFIDELITY AT A GLANCE

Percentage of married or married and cohabiting people who had more than one sexual partner in the last year. This chart is not comprehensive or definitive. Not all the numbers are exactly comparable.

Country	Men	Women
Togo (1998)	37.0	0.5
Cameroon (2004)	36.5	4.4
Ivory Coast (1998)	36.1	1.9

Country	Men	Women
Mozambique (2003)	28.9	3.1
Tanzania (2005)	27.6	2.6
Haiti (2000)	25.4	0.8
Benin (2001)	23.4	0.6
Zambia (2002)	22.6	1.5
Uganda (2001)	22.3	1.2
Burkina Faso (2003)	20.1	0.5
China urban (2000)	18.3	3.2
Dominican Republic (2002)	18	0.8
Mexico City (2001)	15	n/a
Zimbabwe (1999)	13.8	0.7
Peru (1996)	13.5	0.1
Ghana (2003)	13.0	0.4
Brazil (1996)	12.0	0.8
Kenya (2003)	11.5	1.6
Norway (1997)	10.8	6.6
China (2000)	10.5	n/a
Great Britian***	9.3	5.1
Bolivia (2003)	8.6	0.4
Ethiopia (2000)	6.9	1.0
Armenia (2000)	4.7	0.1
Philippines (2003)	4.5	0.0
U.S.A. (2004)*	3.9	3.1
France (2004)**	3.8	2.0
Italy (1998)	3.5	0.9
Rwanda (2000)	3.2	0.1

lies, damn lies, and adultery

Country	Men	Women
Niger (1998)	27.2	0.1
Nigeria (2003)	15.2	0.6
Chad (2004)	19.9	0.7
Malawi (2000)	16.3	0.5
Mali (2001)	22.4	0.7
Namibia (2000)	13.0	1.2
Nepal (2001)	3.0	0
Switzerland (1997)	3.0	1.1
Australia (2002)	2.5	1.8
Kazakhstan (1999)	1.6	0.9
Bangladesh (2004)	1.6	n/a

*married only, ages 18 and older

**married only, ages 18–54

***married and cohabititing, ages 16–44

Sources: General Social Survey, 2005; China Health and Family Life Survey; MEA-SURE DHS (2006) Demographic and Health Surveys, 1984–present; EU New Encounter Module Project (2006) NEM surveys; Smith, M. A., C. E. Rissel, et al. (2003), "The Rationale and Methods of the Australian Study of Health and Relationships," *Australian and New Zealand Journal of Public Health* 27(2): 106–116; calculations by Emma Slaymaker, London School of Hygiene & Tropical Medicine; Beltzer N., M. Lagarde, et al., Les connaissances, attitudes, croyances et comportements face au VIH/sida en France—Evolutions 1992–1994–1998–2001 et 2004, rapport de l'ORS Ile-de-France, novembre 2005, p. 204; National Survey of Sexual Attitudes and Lifestyles II, 2000–2001.

EXTRAMARITAL SEX IN AMERICA

Percentage of married Americans over age 18 who've had more than one sex partner in the last 12 months

	Men	*Women*	*All*
1988	5.0	2.8	3.9
1989	5.8	1.7	3.6
1990	5.3	2.3	3.8
1991	5.4	3.4	4.4
1993	4.1	1.9	2.9
1994	3.6	1.3	2.4
1996	5.2	2.5	3.8
1998	4.9	2.5	3.6
2000	5.6	2.3	3.8
2002	4.3	1.9	3.0
2004	3.9	3.1	3.5

Source: General Social Survey.

THREE

sexual cultures

IN THEORY, a university-educated white woman (like me) could date and marry an immigrant Mexican laborer who didn't finish high school. But although I occasionally meet working-class Mexicans, we seem to exist in separate romantic zones. Our chances of dating or getting married are practically nil. Like most Americans, I have had romantic partners who shared my ethnicity, schooling, and economic standing. Even when they weren't American, my boyfriends have been stock analysts and journalists.

The way we sort our sex partners intrigued researchers at the University of Chicago. They wondered how a Mexican man in Chicago, a city of 3 million people, might find that every potential girlfriend he meets comes from the same town in Michoacán. Meanwhile my girlfriends gripe that all the eligible men they know are lawyers from New Jersey.

National sex statistics reveal only so much about a place. In fact, every neighborhood consists of crisscrossing "sexual cultures" that shape people's expectations about whom to court, how sexual relationships progress, and when and whether to be faithful. A sexual culture is an amalgam of all the individual rules I talked about earlier—both the official and the unofficial ones. These rules are influenced by how much money people have, what their physical landscapes are like, and the kinds of institutions—schools, companies, courts of law—that have a say in their sexual behavior. The boundaries of a sexual culture can be as big as a country or as narrow as a law firm, a construction site, a lesbian clique, or an Internet chat room. Most of us move between several. A gay man who works at an investment bank probably moves between two different sexual cultures every day. What's crucial is that everyone in a particular sexual culture knows its rules and has a stake in following them.

But how are we routed into a sexual culture, and how do we learn its rules? Does someone enforce them? How does a sexual culture change over time? Do the media play a role?

Between 1995 and 1997, researchers led by Edward Laumann, a sociologist at the University of Chicago, mapped sexual habits in four Chicago neighborhoods. They focused on neighborhoods within driving distance of each other: an African-American district in south Chicago where most people weren't educated beyond high school; an affluent neighborhood of young whites and gays along Chicago's North Shore; a western neighborhood of mostly working-class Mexican immigrants and their families; and another Spanish-speaking area populated by people with Puerto Rican and Mexican origins. They also interviewed a representative sample of people from the whole city and nearby suburbs to compare with the neighborhood findings.

Their results, published in "The Sexual Organization of the City," show that different sexual cultures cross each other without anyone getting confused about what their own rules are or even being more than vaguely aware of what people just across town, or sitting next to them on a commuter train, are doing. Hooking up with strangers is difficult enough. People preferred their potential sex partners to be vetted by someone they knew, or by a school or church they also attended. Even just having acquaintances in common made them more likely to end up in bed together.

Nearly half of heterosexual men in the white neighborhood, which the researchers dubbed "Shoreland," had met their most recent sex partner at school or work. This isn't surprising, since many Shorelanders were recent college graduates who had moved into the area in the last year. Shorelanders also tended to spend a lot of time working (interviewers had a hard time finding them at home or getting access to their high-rise apartments).

None of the gay men in the same neighborhood had met their last partner at school, and only 9 percent said they'd met their last partner at work. However, they'd had much more success in bars and nightclubs, where 50 percent said they'd met their most recent partner.

Gay bars and nightclubs were a good place to arrange flings, whereas schools and workplaces routed straight men into longer-term romances. Forty-three percent of gay men said they'd had more than sixty sex partners in their adult lives, compared to 4 percent of straight men in the same neighborhood who said so. (This big difference isn't fully explained by the fact that Shoreland's straight men tended to be younger.) Indeed, most straight men seemed monastic compared to their gay neighbors: More than a third of straight men had slept with five or fewer people in their lifetimes (just 2 percent of gay men said that).

The researchers found that people sometimes conveyed the rules of a sexual culture by telling "causal stories" about the harm that comes from certain sexual behaviors. Some Christian groups, for instance, warn that even a one-night stand can damage a relationship many years later. Something as mundane as the price of real estate shapes a sexual culture. So do the ratio of men to women and whether family members live nearby. Merely having access to a car can dramatically transform a person's sexual prospects, too.

In the Mexican neighborhood, which researchers called "Westside," many residents lived with their extended families. Westsiders were more likely than residents of the other areas to have met their most recent partner in a relative's home. Women in Westside had an especially hard time meeting anyone else, since they were the least likely of any group in the study to have access to cars. Westside women lived an average of three miles from their most recent partner, compared with the all-Chicago average of ten miles. That is, they mostly paired up with people to whose homes they could walk.

In the African-American neighborhood, dubbed "Southtown," the most common meeting places were public settings like parks and city streets. Although the typical Southtown resident had lived in the neighborhood at least ten years and had at least half his family in Chicago, not a single black man said he'd met his most recent partner in a relative's house. In fact, about 40 percent of Southtown men said they went outside their neighborhood to meet women. The women left behind went to church more frequently than any other group in the survey; perhaps they were praying for love.

In Southtown, economics influenced whether people were monogamous. Half were unemployed at the time of the survey. And because Southtown's women were better educated, the jobless tended to be men. That meant that men with jobs were a scarce commodity, and the men knew it. Some 39 percent of Southtown men said they'd had at least two overlapping sexual relationships during the last year. Twenty-seven percent said they'd kept two sexual relationships going at once for six months or longer, a practice the researchers call "long-term polygamy."

The researchers speculate that black women put up with this because employed men with other girlfriends were more appealing than faithful men without jobs. Just 8 percent of Southtown women said they'd had concurrent partners in the last year, though 20 percent said their partners had been with other women.

Once black men in Chicago got married, they were as monogamous as whites (97 percent had had only one partner in the last year). But few made it to the altar, since, as the researchers explain, long-term polygamy isn't conducive to marriage. Far fewer blacks than whites in the whole Chicago area were married. Chicago's highly educated black men over thirty-five, who presumably had the best jobs and were therefore the most attractive to women, were the least likely to be married.

Only gay and straight men in the white neighborhood, Shoreland, came close to matching Southtown's infidelity rates. But these men favored "short-term polygamy"—overlapping relationships that last less than six months. Southtown men managed several serious relationships simultaneously. Shorelanders presumably dated a few people at once before getting more serious with one of them, or they had a main squeeze and flings on the side. This pattern is more apt to lead to marriage. And once they got married, whites—like blacks—were highly monogamous.

For those prizing fidelity above all else, Spanish-speaking women were the best bet. Just 2 percent of women in the Mexican and Puerto Rican areas said they'd had overlapping sex partners in the last year. The women were probably limited by the fact that they lived with members of their extended families, who watched them closely. Even Mexican men were a lower adultery risk than the lawyers I'm used to. Perhaps I should have given some of them my number.

THE CHICAGO STUDY describes how one city contains lots of different sexual cultures. But what about the way a single sexual culture changes over time? To see how this works, I visited women in their seventies living in "retirement communities" in Florida. Speaking to this group of friends is like visiting a different America. Although their extramarital heyday was in the 1950s and 1960s and many of their affair partners have died, the women say the affairs were the best times of their lives.

Americans who are now having affairs, or recovering from them, all asked me to change their names. But the women in Florida begged me to use their real names; they weren't at all ashamed of their youthful adventures. (I changed their names anyway.) "We didn't have guilt then," one of them tells me. "Everybody knew. It was exciting. It was thrilling!"

The women spent most of their lives in an affluent, mostly white town in New Jersey, across the George Washington Bridge from Manhattan. Over the last ten years, they and their surviving husbands have migrated south to the area around Palm Beach.

Their sexual culture was shaped by the postwar world in which they lived. They were a bit young for the wave that swept women into the workforce; few had full-time jobs. Most had live-in maids and the occasional summer in the south of France. Their sons were supposed to become doctors. Their husbands manufactured ladies' sportswear or presided over small dry-cleaning empires. On birthdays and anniversaries, the women got important jewelry. The main thing was, they got married, most of them by age twenty-two. "My mother used to say, 'The only place a woman can go by herself is the toilet.' You had to be married," Loretta, now sixty-eight, tells me.

Unlike their mothers, the women in Loretta's social circle were restless. The economic boom that followed World War II had made them richer than their parents. Instead of a comfortable life with a husband they'd known since high school, they craved glamour and romance. "We all learned from the movie stars," says Loretta, who married three times and now lives in Lake Worth, Florida. "New York then was like long black gloves and little hats, and you met your sweetheart in New York for a drink, kind of thing. It was like Sinatra and stuff like that. The songs had words, and you closed your eyes."

Barb, seventy-seven, whose dress shop was the town's gossip hub, talks about her former customers as if they were still coming through the door. She speaks as they all do, in a thick New Jersey accent:

"There was one woman who used to come to the store and look at her watch, 'Is it one o'clock?' She would meet him every day at one o'clock."

"Helen was the wife of a carpenter. Yvonne had an affair with [him]."

"Linda was the only woman that ever shopped in Bloomingdale's at midnight, 'cause that's what she told her husband. Just think of a disgusting-looking shipping clerk. She would just have affair after affair."

"Alice was sort of happily married, but not. There was a surprise birthday party, and that afternoon she's screwing someone in a hotel room. So they had an affair, and then her husband got a letter. She moved out with her two children."

"Bob, he had an affair with Judy's husband's secretary."

"I think most people knew Les's wife had an affair for many years."

"It was Peyton Place there," explains Barb, who now lives in an "active adult community" in Lake Worth. "And I found out that in Long Island, from the women here, it was the same."

Since the statistics don't go back that far, it's impossible to know if women of Barb's milieu had more affairs in the 1960s than comparable women do today. In the national sex survey published in 1994, about 12 percent of women born in the 1930s said they'd ever had extramarital sex—less than women from the two subsequent generations. However, 37 percent of men born in the 1930s said they'd had extramarital sex, substantially more than men born anytime after that.

At its peak the New Jersey women's sexual culture may have encompassed only a handful of country clubs. But the stories they tell illustrate how much a sexual culture changes over time. These days an adulteress might swear a few close friends to secrecy. But the women in New Jersey told strings of girlfriends about their love affairs and sometimes introduced their lovers—who were potential second husbands—to their mothers. In any case, they say it was easy to guess who was "going out to lunch" with whom.

There were plenty of opportunities to cheat. At country clubs, charitable events, and house parties, married people flirted and danced while their spouses were in the next room. And since many of the wives in this group had round-the-clock baby-sitters and no jobs (or at least none of the sixty-hours-a-week variety), they had plenty of free time.

These women can't believe how uptight people from the younger generations are about these matters. Some of the women's own children are so resentful they don't speak to their mothers. "Things are different now. Our children in their forties are repelled by that," says Loretta. The women know better than to reminisce about the good old days with anyone besides each other.

And now with me. I arrange to meet two of Barb's friends, Elaine and Nancy, at the spa in Pompano Beach, Florida, where they're taking a little holiday. They tell me to arrive anytime before their four o'clock massages. When I get to the restaurant where they're having lunch, they immediately size me up. Though I'm four decades their junior, I can see them mentally comparing me to their younger selves and deciding that they could have outdone me. Elaine is a seventy-three-year-old widow, *Dynasty* chic, with giant black glasses, a diamond watch, and a floor-length red dress that stretches over her bathing suit and ample bosom. Nancy, seventy-five, has blue eyes, high cheekbones, and is wearing gold shorts that show off her impressively smooth legs.

There's a brief dispute over who gets to tell her story first. For both women, affairs were the great adventures of their lives. "I'm talking about going to meet him in New York one day and having detectives follow me and having them chase me!" says Nancy, who looks a bit like Lauren Bacall. She first spotted Larry, a married real-estate developer, as he walked off the golf course. "The sun is setting behind him. He has the bluest eyes that I have ever seen."

Nancy beams as she describes how she conspired to join Larry on a business trip to Canada. "I told my husband that I was going to visit a friend in Florida, and he said 'Okay, take a couple of days and go to Florida.' So I went to Montreal. . . . I had to go and find a spa and go to a tanning room and get a tan. And the way it was arranged was that when my husband called my friend in Florida, her mother answered and said, 'Oh, the girls are on the beach.'"

Women in subsequent generations increasingly had jobs, so they could walk away from their marriages without having anyone else waiting in the wings. But in the 1960s, women like Elaine and Nancy traded one husband for another. Though some of their affairs began as sideline romances, all of the women I speak to eventually married their affair partners and then, they say, remained faithful to them. They went straight from the care of their fathers to the care of a succession of husbands. While their divorces were being finalized, their future husbands would put them and their children up in apartments.

Perhaps because these men were meant to be Prince Charmings, there's an exaggerated, storybook quality to these romances, with thunderstruck moments and breathless hours waiting by the telephone. When Elaine met Irwin in the late

1950s, it was a cross between a supermarket romance and *Fiddler on the Roof*:

"I went to a party at my uncle's house, who was a dentist in town. Somehow or other I see this guy across a crowded room. It sounds corny, but he came to me, and I went to him and looked at him, and I knew this was mine, this was for me . . . and he said, 'Meet me tonight in New York.'"

Elaine was then twenty-five years old. "I said, 'I don't even know how to drive into New York myself. . . . I can't meet you tonight.' My grandmother was at this party. My mother and father were at this party. But I knew I was going to meet him."

A few days later, Elaine got dressed up, left her children with the maid, and drove to Chandler's, a restaurant on East Forty-sixth Street in Manhattan. When Irwin arrived, she was already posed in a banquette. Elaine recalls that Irwin said, "You know, I don't do this where I *live.* I don't know what made me do it, but I had to see you."

At this point in the story, Elaine pauses. "You don't want the details of the sexual part of it, do you?" she asks.

"Well, we had dinner. And I said to myself, 'If I'm going to do this, I'm gonna do it. . . . We got in the car, and we just kissed and sat there. And I went down on him, in the car! I did! And he was in shock. I said to myself, 'If I'm going to do it, I'm going to do it the whole way!'"

Their affair became a regular thing. "He told me, 'I am never going to marry you. This is the whipped cream and the cherry on top of the sundae. I'm never going to marry you but we're going to have a wonderful time.'

"Well, that wasn't good enough for me, and I got more friendly with his wife, so that the four of us were together constantly; we were always together. There were times when Irwin and I were in New York and we'd fall asleep in a hotel, and we'd both be late coming home, and we had dates that night [with each other], and the husband and wife never put it together. His wife didn't care, as long as he was there to take her out to dinner."

Barb, who owned the dress shop, remembers that Elaine would go shopping with Irwin's wife. "Then she'd see him at night and say, 'Ugh, what your wife bought!'"

Elaine's mother was furious when she learned Elaine planned to marry Irwin, but her father slipped her cash and her friends were supportive. They already knew Irwin and liked him. Barb helped Elaine move out of her husband's house. "We left him a bed, a TV, a coffeemaker, and a cup and saucer," Barb recalls.

Elaine's doubts about ditching her husband for her lover were assuaged by her rabbi, whom she describes as "a brilliant man." "I said, 'Rabbi Stein, I'm going to leave my husband, and I'm not sure I'm doing the right thing. I'm worried because I'm destroying so many lives around me, I think.' And he said, 'No, my dear, if you stay, you're destroying their lives. If you go, you'll save all their lives.' . . . And I ran out, I was like flying. . . . He was quite a guy, that Rabbi Stein. Of course, he was divorced himself."

During Bill Clinton's impeachment trial, people often wondered how America got to a point where a president's sexual behavior was the public's business. They often pointed out that when John Kennedy was president in the early 1960s, he had lots of extramarital affairs and there was no public fuss.

Kennedy was living in the same sexual culture that the women I met in Florida once inhabited. He and his celebrity cronies probably helped to create it. But even Kennedy was a product of his times. Not only were women then usually financially dependent on their husbands, it was also harder to divorce (especially for a Roman Catholic). What's more, respectable people around him were cheating, too. Had Kennedy lived a few more years, he might have run into Henry Hyde, the future leader of the Clinton impeachment trial, with his mistress Cherie Snodgrass at a Chicago supper club. There's a picture of Snodgrass and Hyde out in public together, all dressed up and posing for the camera. When Hyde defended his "youthful indiscretions," what he probably meant, yet couldn't say, was that it was simply another era.

A SEXUAL CULTURE isn't a police state; usually no one goes around issuing tickets. So who enforces the rules? An American sociologist named Steven Ortiz set out to answer this question by studying the mobile "adultery culture" created by major-league baseball players while they're on the road. Ortiz, who teaches at Oregon State University, spent three years traveling with various teams (he won't say which ones) and then published some of his findings in a paper called "Traveling with the Ball Club."

Typically a few wives travel with a team on any given trip. Some are regulars, and others join their husbands occasionally. This arrangement leaves open the possibility that the wives who travel with the team will go home and tell other wives what they've seen. At the very least they could interfere with a team's good time on the road.

To avoid this, the players first delineate physical spaces where wives aren't welcome. On the chartered airplanes the teams use to travel to away games, wives sit up front and aren't allowed to linger in the back of the plane. Players sit in the back of the plane, where they're free to flirt with female flight attendants and bond with each other before the game. No one tells the wives they're not wanted, but the women get the message when players taunt them as they pass by or when a gregarious group suddenly clams up as they approach. The newbie wife who plops down next to her husband for a chat is met with silence and a "glaring look of disapproval" from his teammates. As a wife named Stacy explains, "I'm even hesitant, when I use the bathroom, to look right or left and even converse with anyone, because I know that [the players are] there together. . . ." (Ortiz changed the names of the wives.)

If that's not unwelcoming enough, the flight attendants make it clear they resent having the wives on board. "You'd ask for something, and they would slam the Pepsi down on your tray or slide your dinner over to you," explains a wife named Robyn. The animosity is mutual, since some of the wives said they knew that several players had had affairs with attendants they met on team flights.

Players mark out their sexual territory more explicitly when they arrive at the hotel. In many cases they tell their wives not to enter the bar at the team's hotel. Players also tell their wives which other bars, discos, and restaurants in the city are off-limits. This list changes from one season to the next. The players spell this out, instead of hoping their wives just intuit it, because they want to create a safe zone where players whose wives aren't with them can mingle with sports "groupies" (who know to congregate in the hotel bar) and where they can bring their girlfriends without fear of being observed.

Some of the athletes, particularly the more famous ones, don't want to be discreet around the team. Their status rises when other players see them with attractive groupies. By having sex with a groupie, a player is showing he's a man—and a teammate—before he's a husband, Ortiz says. The players prefer to meet groupies at the hotel bar rather than someplace else so that other players will see them doing it.

Usually it's the wives who have to keep a low profile. Some wives say that if they see a married player with a woman who's not his wife, they look away and pretend not to have noticed. One describes how she faced the wall and tried to become "invisible" when she found herself riding a hotel elevator with a married player and a local woman. "If you acknowledge the fact, and if you even show any disapproval of it, then you won't go on any more trips because they'll tell your husband, 'Your wife better keep her mouth shut,'" says Sheila. Some of the wives say they try hard to believe that the woman in question is "a visiting female relative, female family friend, or sister-in-law."

Of course, it's another story if it's the media who catch a player cheating. Then he's obliged to switch to the adultery script for ordinary people, in order to be absolved by the public. According to *Sports Illustrated,* Los Angeles Lakers star Kobe Bryant "had to choke back tears" during a 2003 press conference where he admitted to a tryst with a nineteen-year-old woman in a hotel room. As his wife "gripped his hand and stared into his eyes" Bryant told reporters, "I sit here before you guys furious at myself, disgusted at myself for making the mistake of adultery." (Ortiz followed professional basketball players, too, and found that they had similar rules to those of baseball players while on the road.)

Not all players enforce the codes equally. Ortiz finds that those with the lowest status—low-paid newcomers, players with injuries or in a professional slump—are the strictest about policing the rules, presumably because they feel most vulnerable. The best players have more leeway. One woman recounts how a team star ignored her protests and insisted on taking her and another wife into the hotel bar for a drink. Once inside, despite their celebrity escort, the woman says she "looked straight ahead at the counter, feeling very uncomfortable."

Why do the wives obey these rules, which are personally demeaning and could help their own husbands cheat when they're not there? Why don't the wives just band together and mutiny so that none of their husbands can get away with cheating?

One reason is money. If they make a fuss or break the rules, they might jeopardize their husbands' standing on the team. Athletes' careers aren't long, and the traveling wives usually don't work. Any challenge to their husbands' status is also a threat to a couple's livelihood. Ortiz doesn't cite any instances where a player was demoted or fired because of something his wife did, but the mere threat of poisoning a husband's reputation seems to help keep the women in line.

A tattletale wife also risks becoming a persona non grata. Team members are friendly to wives who are known to be "cool," but they shun women known as "blabbers" and will pressure a player to keep his talkative wife at home. A wife who can't travel with the team loses the chance to keep an eye on her own husband at least part of the time, and she loses out on the glamour and perks of being part of a major-league team. A wife's reputation follows her even when her husband changes teams. "The more you talk, the less people trust you because it's like everyone's doing it," says a wife named Olivia. "For those wives who have told things they've seen, they're like the plague. Nobody wants to be around them."

Rather than banding together, the wives themselves help enforce the rules that allow men to cheat. They discourage each other from gossiping about what they've seen on the road, out of fear that a few blabbers will tar them all as "talkers." Some also don't want to know what their own husbands are doing. When a wife gossips, others will gossip about *her,* saying she's trying to cover for problems in her own marriage.

The genius of this sexual culture is that eventually the wives change from following the rules because they have to, to following them because they want to. Even though they're opposed to adultery, they come to believe that rules permitting affairs are intrinsically significant. Ortiz says, "Most wives firmly believe that it is important not to tell the wife of a philandering husband what they have seen."

THERE'S ANOTHER KIND of sexual culture that doesn't occupy a physical space, and whose members often don't even know each other. It exists in that realm known as "the media." America has a healthy tabloid press, but nowhere have the media carved out a freestanding sexual culture the way they have in Britain. The country's top-selling Sunday newspapers, *News of the World* and the *Mail on Sunday,* frequently devote their entire front sections to tales of adultery. It's as if cheating is the country's biggest news.

In their own lives, Britons react to affairs much the way Americans do. They tend to assume that infidelity is grounds for divorce, or at least for a crisis. They have about the same proportion of extramarital affairs as people in other wealthy countries.

But Britons have another sexual culture that exists only in the media. This one treats adultery as a sport. The game is to catch someone famous in a compromising position. Reporters search through garbage cans if they have to. Tabloids are so desperate for fresh tales of cheating that when they don't have the goods on someone truly famous, they settle for stories on deposed reality-television "stars," C-list actors, and ordinary Britons stuck in bizarre love triangles.

A typical cover story in the *Sun,* Britain's top-selling daily, describes the travails of "two-timed Amy Nuttall," a twenty-two-year-old soap-opera actress who confesses she vandalized the flat of her ex-boyfriend, Ben, an actor on the same series. The sympathetic writer explains that Amy had "hit the roof when she learned Ben had sex in a car with star-struck bank girl Jenny Woodcock, 19, after he approached her in a night-club." To make matters worse, the *Sun* reports, "Amy had to endure Jenny's newspaper revelations about the encounter, in which she branded Ben a lousy lover." In a posed cover photograph, Amy wears a brown string bikini. The article mentions she's hoping to launch a singing career.

Other headlines range from the playful ("Trucking Rat Keeps Going Haul the Way") to the freakish ("My Designer Vagina Ruined My Life," which goes on to explain that "with her new-found confidence came promiscuity—Denize just couldn't keep her brand new privates, er . . . private").

Some tabloid stories might moralize a bit, but readers know that they're meant to be playful. Serious reporting is left to television and a handful of smaller newspapers. To make sure that readers stay interested, tabloid accounts of infidelity are written languourously, with heated details of the alleged "offenses." Whenever possible, they include photographs of either the culprit or the victim clad in a swimsuit.

Some of the tabloid "news" is entirely manufactured. Publicist Max Clifford is the first stop for people with a story to tell, or those hoping to drum one up. As Clifford explains in the *Financial Times*, "What happens now is that young girls will go out to clubs with targets. Such-and-such a footballer is worth

X, and such-and-such a footballer is worth *Y.* My office has calls from young girls asking, 'If we were to choose between *X* and *Y,* who'd be the biggest name?' It's as calculating as that." Clifford gets 20 percent of a newspaper's fees.

Occasionally the tabloids commit themselves to what is, at least in relative terms, a higher purpose: They go after public officials. The point of these attacks isn't to improve policymaking, it's to puncture any hint of sanctimony. When John Major became Britain's prime minister in 1990, the newspapers had a rare opportunity. At the annual conference of Major's Conservative Party in 1993, the government was desperate to distract the public from a recession and launched what it called a "Back to Basics" campaign. This was ostensibly about emphasizing education, but the underlying message—and the behind-the-scenes briefings—made it clear that Conservatives wanted to resuscitate Britain's supposedly waning family values.

Tabloids took "Back to Basics" as an invitation to pry into the lives of Conservative politicians. The resulting sex scandals unfolded quickly. Stephen Milligan, a member of Parliament, was found dead in his apartment wearing women's stockings and with a plastic bag over his head, apparently following an autoerotic act. The Earl of Caithness, a junior minister, resigned after his wife's suicide proved to have been prompted by his affair with a former secretary. Environment Minister Tim Yeo, who now writes a golf column, admitted he'd fathered a child by his mistress. Roads Minister Stephen Morris was discovered to have five mistresses ("Yes, Yes, Yes, Yes, Yes, Minister," the *Daily Telegraph* joked, a play on the television comedy

Yes, Minister). Heritage Secretary David Mellor resigned after his mistress, a fledgling actress named Antonia de Sancha, told newspapers that he liked sucking her toes while she wore the uniform of Chelsea, his favorite soccer team. Soon the national joke was that instead of "Back to Basics," the party's slogan should be "Back to My Place."

Even John Major, whom people dubbed "the gray man" because he was so dull and who was depicted on the satirical television program *Spitting Image* as an all-gray puppet eating peas with his wife, Norma, turned out to have blemishes. These were revealed by Edwina Currie, a former health minister who, as it happens, was keeping a diary while she had a four-year extramarital affair with Major in the 1980s.

I meet Currie in London at a restaurant near Victoria Station to try to understand Britain's tabloid press and the sexual culture it conjures. Not only has Currie, now fifty-nine, been party to a sex scandal involving a prime minister but, since losing her parliamentary seat in 1997, she's developed a new career writing novels about political sex scandals. Currie is no demure English rose. She's a small woman with heavy brown eyebrows and a thicket of reddish hair. She is articulate and extremely opinionated.

"One of the better British values is modesty, so if you are a good guy, you don't go around telling everybody. The instant somebody does, the press are very interested, and he will be followed for weeks on end, and they will end up knowing more about him than he knows about himself."

She says Americans idealize their leaders and are surprised

when they turn out to have messy personal lives. However, Britons enjoy seeing their heroes tumble and assume that there's some sleaze behind every squeaky-clean image. If this turns out to be wrong, they're disappointed.

"Americans, I think, strike us like rather innocent teenagers: full of energy and vigor and pumping red blood but actually not too sure what to do about it. Europe is mature, sophisticated, laid back, and a bit deadpan. That's why, when a politician in Britain stands up and says 'back to basics, family values,' the rest of the nation says, 'Yeah, we'll agree with that, but let's just find out what you did last Sunday afternoon.'"

Next to the staged stories about actresses and soccer stars, Currie's affair with Major seems very human. In the 1980s both were part of the wave of young Conservative MPs swept into power during the so-called Thatcher Revolution. Both were from modest backgrounds, and both wanted to supplant the upper-class fogies who had always controlled the party. They were co-conspirators. "We had rather similar sorts of patterns going in. And we got friendly," Currie tells me.

When they met at a flat near Parliament, Major always clutched an official brown envelope to use as an alibi if anyone stopped him. When Currie complained about her political struggles to her husband, he'd just tell her to quit. But Major was fighting the same battles. "You gain a lot of support and friendship and love from a relationship that is very strengthening," she says.

Currie says she ended the affair in 1988, after both had risen through the party ranks, Currie to health minister and Major to chief secretary to the treasury. She gripes in her diary that success had changed him. "It was best when he was restless, hiding himself, lacked confidence; he told me about his family, his early background, about being out of work, nearly being killed in an accident, all the deep things you only tell your soul. . . ."

When Major became prime minister in 1990, Currie expected him to make her a minister again—based on her qualifications, not their romantic history—but the call never came. ("To be forgotten by someone you'd been sleeping with only eighteen months ago is very, very hard.") Then Currie watched the political explosion that followed "Back to Basics," all the while knowing that Major's own "family values" were challenged. She probably could have brought down the government.

That's when Currie and Major's companionable affair became the stuff of future tabloid journalism, a transformation that, given Britain's sexual culture, seemed inevitable even to Currie. "I knew I was going to tell sooner or later. When you're involved with something as important as an affair with someone who becomes prime minister, you always feel that it's not your information to withhold. At some point you will hand it over as public knowledge." Currie waited until the Conservatives and Major lost power on their own, and until she and her first husband divorced. In 2002 the *Times* published excerpts from her diaries. This kiss-and-tell has made Currie a celebrity. While I'm sitting with her, several young women approach our table to tell her she's "an inspiration."

Just like Chicagoans, people in Britain don't get confused

about which sexual culture they belong to. The one conjured by tabloid newspapers is an adjunct to real life. No one expects to live by its zany rules. That is, no one who isn't a politician or a reality-television star. Like Edwina Currie, those people might assume that whatever happens in their bedrooms is ultimately the public's business.

America has its own forum where adultery is discussed and scrutinized every day. But, unlike the one in Britain, America's forum does change the way its ordinary citizens behave. It's what I call "the marriage-industrial complex."

the marriage-industrial complex

OPENING NIGHT AT the Smart Marriages Conference in Dallas feels like a carnival. In a room the size of a football field, entrepreneurs stand in booths and shout over the mariachi band about their remedies for fixing broken marriages. If I dare to make eye contact as I walk past, they rush forward, thrust brochures and CD-ROMs at me, and launch into their sales pitches.

"We have a very structured process which includes mirroring, but then validation and empathy, so beyond just mirroring you get into something really connecting," the executive director of Imago Relationships International yells over the trumpet. Others want to teach me "How to Avoid Marrying a Jerk" or how to "Laugh Your Way to a Better Marriage." Some of the sellers are professional therapists, while others are former stand-up comics and management consultants who have gotten into the marriage business.

I never realized how many different things could go wrong in a marriage until I saw all these cures. I've been married less than a year myself, but I'm depressed by the mere thought of one day paying a former sitcom writer to "rattle" my "marriage brain" or, worse, needing a two-day workshop in "Hot Monogamy."

The dozens of remedies available here are part of America's marriage-industrial complex, the sum of all the TV shows, self-help books, and tens of thousands of couples counselors whose raison d'être is to explain why relationships go wrong. The topic of infidelity runs through the whole marriage-industrial complex. There are weekly support groups for cuckolded spouses and "sex addicts"; Web sites for adulterers, their mates and mistresses; healing weekends for couples in the throes of an infidelity crisis; and themed destinations like the Affair Recovery Center in Austin, Texas. These entrepreneurs have taken America's adultery script and written in their own message: Beware. Do not attempt to manage this on your own.

At the Smart Marriages Conference, a row of infidelity booths occupy prime real estate in the front of the hall. Anne and Brian Bercht, who until recently were merely an organizer of business seminars and a building contractor, respectively, are promoting their new memoir, *My Husband's Affair* Became *the Best Thing That Ever Happened to Me.* The book has already landed Brian an appearance on *The Oprah Winfrey Show* and has launched the couple's new vocation as motivational speakers on the topic of marriage, relationships, and affairs.

Brand is king here. Michele Weiner-Davis, a social worker whose assistants man her busy booth, still recalls the moment she came up with a name for her approach to couples therapy. "I remember sitting in my home office, and all of a sudden I thought, 'Divorce busters, *divorce busting!*'" she says. "I just knew I had hit on something that would really change my life." Soon afterward some reporters showed up at a talk she gave under the "Divorce Busting" title. Offers to write a book and appearances on television shows soon followed. Weiner-Davis, fifty-two, now heads a small empire that includes books, counseling, and speaking engagements around the country. A photograph of her looking determined and optimistic appears on every page of her Web site. Her mantra is that almost every marriage is salvageable, even after infidelity and even if only one spouse wants to work things out. She says people can get their straying spouses back by acting confident instead of crumbling. The cover of her *Divorce Busting* book promises results within a month. "Practically all of my clients are having affairs. A lot of them are," she says.

America's relationship entrepreneurs seem sincere about wanting to help people, but they're also in business. Just as the military-industrial complex needs wars, the marriage-industrial complex needs adulterous couples to believe they require help from professionals. If people think they can handle it alone—as they used to in America, and as they still do in most of the world—the entrepreneurs are out of a job.

The marriage-industrial complex has largely succeeded. Even Americans who scoff at self-help books and would never hire a "relationship tele-coach" spout the wisdom of the marriage-industrial complex anyway, without knowing where it originated. It has come to seem obvious to Americans that the discovery of infidelity leads to a confrontation, followed by counseling, perhaps other forms of support, and a long period of discussion and recovery (sometimes in perpetuity). Americans absorb this chronology through magazine articles, television shows, and advice from friends. If you've ever sat your partner down to discuss your relationship, or if you believe that after your wife cheats on you it's best to talk about what happened, or if you treat infidelity as a problem that can be solved, the marriage-industrial complex has gotten to you.

ANGELA IS WATCHING as I speak to her husband, Hank. Or, more precisely, she's hovering. She won't let me speak to him unless she's there. I'm not sure if she thinks I'll seduce him or if she just wants to monitor his story. She wedges herself between the two of us on the couch and rests her arm protectively around him.

Hank, fifty-two, is an appealing guy. He's built like a linebacker but has the gentle manner and easy laugh of someone you'd like to have a beer with. Only that won't happen, because Hank no longer drinks. He's not a recovering alcoholic; he's a recovering adulterer. "I will be someone who has committed adultery until the day I die," he tells me.

Hank remembers exactly where he was standing in the Pittsburgh airport when he was leaving a message on his home answering machine and called his wife by the name of his mistress. That slip opened a new chapter in his life that included quitting his job as a sales manager and having a spiritual awakening.

Angela, who's forty-six and pretty, with wavy brown hair and a curvaceous figure, had had a feeling there was something wrong. That feeling, she realizes now, was the Holy Spirit "nudging" her. "I was just praying to know. Specifically, I was praying that it's going to be through a phone call. And it was through a phone call."

The morning after that phone call, back at their house in a suburb of Atlanta, Hank sat across from Angela in his home office and confessed. At a conference out of town, he had rekindled a relationship with an old girlfriend who worked for his company. "What happened was, shortly after we were married I was at a meeting. I was overcome with lust, and we had . . . I was unfaithful to Angela that night." It was apparently just that one night, but he and the woman kept up a strong emotional connection.

That morning, with Angela listening on the line, Hank called the other woman to say it was over. Angela recalls, "She said, 'I just don't understand where this is coming from.' He just kept reiterating that he loved me and that he was going to stay with me."

Hank didn't stop with his confession to Angela. He also told members of his "men's group" and leaders of his church. They arranged for him to meet once a week with an "accountability partner"—something like a parole officer for adulterers—who introduced Hank to books like *Personal Holiness in Times of Temptation.*

Hank was getting lots of support, but Angela was floundering. Her first husband had been unfaithful, too, but Hank's affair was a turning point. In her quest to get a handle on things, she read a book that said 92 percent of Americans lie. Her mother revealed that her father had cheated also. As this information rolled in, her worldview began to collapse. "I think my view before was that this earth is good and everyone is good," she tells me. "I guess I really didn't see the selfishness of life."

Couples counseling didn't help. Years after Hank's single slipup, Angela says, "I couldn't get past the pain. I said, 'God, I need someone who can understand me.'" She went to her computer and entered the word "affairs" in a search engine. Peggy Vaughan's Web site popped up. "I was kind of walking out the day I found Peggy's Web site," Angela says. She had a ninety-minute phone counseling session with Vaughan and ordered every one of her books. It was the beginning of Angela's recovery.

Peggy Vaughan is a sixty-nine-year-old grandmother in San Diego who has devoted her life to helping people recover from affairs. It's hard to imagine someone with her blend of do-gooding and workaholism emerging anyplace but the United States. She's up at six-thirty most mornings to respond to e-mails from the East Coast—often desperate missives from people in the early stages of discovery.

Vaughan doesn't have therapeutic training, but she draws on her personal experience. In 1974 her husband, James, confessed he'd been fooling around with other women for seven years. "At first I said it can't be happening, because I thought if he is, I automatically had to divorce him and go back to Mississippi to my parents," she says in a spitfire southern drawl. Instead the Vaughans became adultery pioneers. They published a book in 1980 asserting that affairs aren't a marital death sentence. After nearly a hundred television appearances, Vaughan launched a newsletter about infidelity that eventually grew into the Beyond Affairs Network, a support group for cuckolded spouses with chapters in twenty-eight states. Vaughan says couples should expect to spend "thousands of hours" discussing the affair. She helped Angela understand that her husband suffered from an emotional addiction. "It's very narcissistic behavior. It's an act of pleasure. It's pretty comparable to morphine," Angela says.

Vaughan believes adultery is rampant in America. She quotes Kinsey's estimates on levels of cheating and decides that one partner will have an affair in 80 percent of marriages, which is more than double the most credible scientific estimates. On the one hand, she says, magazines and movies glamorize celebrity affairs and make cheating seem like no big deal. But once it happens, she says Americans are ashamed to tell anyone that their spouses are cheating, and they come to feel increasingly isolated and depressed.

Peggy has made herself the protector of these lost souls. At a talk in Dallas, she says a small line of greeting cards aimed at people involved in extramarital affairs is "disgusting" and that no one should joke about infidelity. A story about the cards ran in a Bethesda newspaper, and it's been circulating on the Internet among horrified advocates for marriage. The newspaper itself ran a follow-up story citing the negative feedback it got from readers. The cards don't exactly make adultery sound glamorous. One meant for the holidays says, "As we celebrate with our families, I will be thinking of you." Another that's intended for a coworker says, "I used to look forward to the weekends but since we met they now seem like an eternity."

IN 1970 there were just three thousand marriage and family therapists in America. Most psychologists and psychiatrists assumed that mining a psyche was such a delicate process that you couldn't do it to two people at once. But the nascent marriage-industrial complex was beginning to converge around the idea that a couple isn't just two separate psyches but rather a "system" with its own history and dynamics. "The relationship" soon emerged as an independent entity that professionals could study. This systems theory assumed that while usually only one spouse had an affair, the other played some role in it, too. Therapists began examining a couple's dynamics for clues and searching each of their childhoods for unresolved conflicts that would explain why one of them cheated.

Meanwhile the rising divorce rate, which peaked in 1979, was making relationship problems a national concern. The number of practicing marriage and family therapists jumped to about twenty-two thousand by 1987, then doubled again in the decade after that.

This notion of "affair as symptom" filtered into America's popular imagination. In the 1989 film *When Harry Met Sally,* Harry tells his best friend Jess that his wife has just left him for a tax attorney:

> JESS: Marriages don't break up on account of infidelity. It's just a symptom that something else is wrong.
> HARRY: Oh really? Well that "symptom" is fucking my wife.

In the 1990s, experts were still refining their ideas on what causes relationship problems. Deborah Tannen's bestseller *You Just Don't Understand* and John Gray's *Men Are from Mars, Women Are from Venus* argued that men and women get tripped up by their different styles of communicating, rather than by their emotional baggage. Some therapists even started blaming the affair on the person who had it, though the culprit could still turn around and blame his own parents.

Then, in 1998, the Clinton-Lewinsky affair thrust infidelity's fledgling experts onto prime time. "Back when I started 20 years ago, you couldn't even find infidelity mentioned in the classic family-therapy texts," the psychologist Don-David Lusterman, author of *Infidelity: A Survival Guide,* told the *New York Times.*

Thanks to the new national sex surveys, there were finally some hard data on affairs. Scientists wrote equations to predict how a "rational actor" would weigh the "total utility" of an affair and measured the importance of things like how often people think about sex and how guilty this makes them feel.

Americans learned that 98 percent of men and 78 percent of women have fantasized about someone other than their spouse and that people who thought about sex every day were 22 percent more likely to have had extramarital sex than people who thought about it only a few times a week. They also discovered that people who enjoyed spending time with their spouse's family were 24 percent less likely to have had extramarital sex.

Therapists concluded anecdotally that "boring" was to the 1990s what "frigid" had been to the 1950s. Husbands weren't having affairs with their sexy young secretaries. Frequently they were taking up with women who were older and uglier than their spouses, but more interesting. *Ladies' Home Journal* advised readers that the way to hold on to a husband isn't to lose weight and buy new lingerie, it's to "read, read, read! And then talk about books, articles, movies, and news together. . . . Remember that a healthy marriage isn't about comfort zones and status quos. If you settle for comfort, your marriage will die."

Increasingly, American couples were hearing these messages in a therapist's office. By 2004 there were over fifty thousand marriage and family therapists in America. An industry group estimates that each year 2.6 percent of all married couples consult them—roughly the same percentage as those who say they've committed adultery in the last year. Psychologists, psychiatrists, and social workers treat couples, too. The new research on affairs has also empowered a growing cadre of "marriage experts" of the sort found at the Smart Marriages Conference. They argued that couples don't need years of therapy but rather practical skills that can be taught over a long weekend. These experts rarely have any scientific proof to back their claims but they offer gushing testimonials from former clients.

In her 2003 book *NOT Just Friends,* the Maryland psychologist Shirley Glass broke the news that people in happy marriages cheat, too. She said that as men and women work long hours together and go on joint business trips, friendships unwittingly evolve into romances. This is true even for people who are having great sex at home. Glass and others also began describing the unconsummated "emotional affairs" their patients were developing at work or on the Internet and keeping secret from their spouses. This shifted the thinking on affairs yet again. Not only are affairs not principally about sex, but you can have an affair without even taking your clothes off. Americans coined a new mantra, which I heard over and over as I toured the country: It's not the sex, it's the lying.

SINCE LYING is the problem, truth telling has become America's cure for infidelity. Many therapists believe that a wife is entitled to ask her husband for the details of every text message and blow job he got from his mistress. The rationale is that the relationship between a husband and wife should be transparent. Some couples create a detailed chronology covering the entire period of the infidelity, even if it lasted for several years. The process stops when the wife can't take it anymore, or when she's satisfied that she's overturned every lie he has told. If any stray lies trickle out after this, the wife may have traumatizing flashbacks.

People in other countries didn't believe me when I told them about America's confession cure. They assumed that knowing the details would make a cuckolded spouse feel worse. But the truth-telling cure has become so widespread in the United States that it's now gospel on Web sites for people with cheating spouses. On the frenetically active SurvivingInfidelity.com, "Erica" says she spent twenty months interrogating her husband about his affair, and then "with the aid of my master calendar, the 1000 + email, the photo albums, visa receipts, and his old expense reports, he and I set out to put all of those 2½ years of infidelity on a timeline."

Members of infidelity Web sites are ruthlessly moralistic. To emphasize their status as victims, they use screen names like "so_lost," "choking" and "15ysfornothing." Their messages to each other read like wartime code: "I'm less than two months post dday, so I'm not very sure we're completely in R, though FWH wants to be."

D-day, or "discovery day," is the day a person discovers the partner's affair. Emotional time is measured from d-day forward. R is "recovery" (or sometimes "the relationship"), and FWH is a "former wayward husband." Other abbreviations include OW ("other woman"), BS ("betrayed spouse"), MOm ("maybe other man"), XOP ("ex–other person"), ONS ("one-night stand"), NC (no contact), SITD (still in the dark), and NPD (narcissistic personality disorder). A "cake man" isn't a pastry chef; he's a husband who wants to have his wife and his mistress, too.

Life is complicated, but the rules on the site are simple. A "wayward husband" must stick to a strict schedule of apologies and repentance. When a woman says she's going to a conference where she will run into her former lover, a site administrator advises her to tell him, "XOP, I'm actively working on my marriage, please do not contact or talk to me on a personal level. Have a nice day."

In real life, Americans use stories to justify their affairs, at least to themselves. But the ethos on these Web sites is that nothing excuses cheating. People who say they're in love with an affair partner are informed they're actually in a semihypnotized state called "the adultery fog." When a married woman from Texas writes to say that she's fallen in love with her ex-fiancé, respondents tell her, "What you're feeling is chemicals. . . . You've got something akin to addiction."

On the Internet everyone is competing for the moral high ground. Members of another Web site, called TOW (The Other Woman) describe their own cocktail of desperation, loneliness, and self-doubt. One woman writes, "I would like to expose my affair, but in an indirect way. . . . I don't want to come right out and tell his W, but I want her to find out. Any suggestions???" Within three days there are seventy-nine responses, ranging from signing her lover's penis with an indelible marker to warnings that "d-days" end badly for "other women" such as herself.

THE WORD "RESTORATION" used to make me think of hardware shops and antique furniture. After spending time with born-again Christians in America, however, I can't hear it without thinking about extramarital sex. Across the country religious Christians have developed their own thriving branch of the marriage-industrial complex, based on the principle that marriages can be "restored" even after an infidelity. God "is in the restoration business. That's what He loves to do most, to restore marriages," says Daryl McCray, a pastor in Kendall Lakes, Florida.

Although the New Testament says adultery is grounds for divorce, Christians in America have made the strategic calculation that unless marriages can survive affairs, it will be hard to dent the more troubling problem of divorce. Gone are the days when a cheating husband was driven out of his church or when preachers would sermonize obliquely about affairs. Churches that had already transformed their Sunday services into self-help seminars are now discussing infidelity directly. To keep unfaithful couples together, Christian counselors blend biblical language with modern therapeutic ideas. "We don't just pray for everyone in the name of Jesus and be done. It's more cognitive behavioral with some metaphysics thrown in there," one tells me.

In her book *Avoiding the Greener Grass Syndrome,* Nancy Anderson, who had an intense love affair with a fellow sales representative and briefly left her husband for her lover, advises readers to ask themselves, *"Would I do this in front of my spouse? And if you're still not sure, ask yourself, Would I do it in front of the Lord?"* Anderson offers guidelines for staying out of the infidelity "danger zone" at work. She recommends not being alone in a car with someone of the opposite sex, always talking about your spouse in positive terms, and avoiding "lingering eye contact." When traveling for business, she suggests asking the hotel clerk to block all adult TV channels. If an attraction with a coworker still manages to penetrate these defenses, readers should "consider a transfer to a different department, a different position, or maybe you should quit. No job is more valuable than your marriage."

Most of the Christian courses are taught by couples like Ben and Ann Wilson of Littleton, Colorado, who decided their own brush with adultery was in fact a religious calling. Ben had just started studying for a divinity degree in Kansas City in 1994 when Ann, now forty-two, admitted she'd had a three-year affair. The story of how they made it through the hellfire and patched their marriage back together is now the basis of "Marriage Restored," which includes a blog, a ten-week course at their evangelical church, and a three-day workshop. A church flyer says the course is for "couples experiencing struggles with intimacy in their marriage," but everyone who shows up knows what they're there to discuss.

When Ben and Ann tell their own story to a class of couples, they try to avoid salacious details and instead emphasize parallels with "God's story of fall and redemption." "You could make it a semipornographic presentation if you want," Ben, forty-four, says. He says he tells couples, "The best thing I did when I found out, I committed to feeling as much pain every day as I could, so the healing did begin." Ben and Ann even offer advice on how to tell the kids. They told theirs that "their mom had sex with another man, and I was mad about it, and it would take us a while to deal with that."

Even for a Christian soldier, it's tough in the adultery trenches. The Wilsons' classes aren't always full, and there's the emotional trauma of retelling their personal story. Ben says, "If in ten years God calls me and says, 'We don't need you to counsel on affairs anymore,' part of me would be relieved."

The most extreme group of antidivorce Christians I found were called Covenant Keepers Inc., based in Tulsa, Oklahoma. Their guiding principle is that marriages shouldn't be broken under almost any circumstances. Adherents go through a process they call "standing" for their marriages. When a woman's husband leaves her or even remarries, she renounces sex with anyone else and fasts and prays for God to send her husband home. About three dozen support groups around the country offer emotional and spiritual help through this process, which can last for years or even decades.

The Bible says adultery is a sin, but Covenant Keepers stress it's a "forgivable" one, since divorce is worse. "We believe that because marriage is a covenant, He truly has created a one-flesh entity. When you divorce, it's literally like taking an arm and ripping it off your body. That's why divorce hurts so much," explains Naomi, who manages the Southeast region for Covenant Keepers from her home in North Carolina.

Naomi had been married sixteen years when her husband, Alfred, left her for a coworker at his information-technology company. She didn't date and still conducted herself "like a married woman," even though she was technically divorced. "All of my friends said to me, 'This man is gone. He's married to someone else.' But God said to me, 'Keep your vow.' And He intends us to do that whether our mate's doing it or not." As for the spiritual destiny of Alfred's new wife, "I realized God had a plan and purpose for her life. It just doesn't include my husband."

After eleven years, Alfred did indeed come home. The couple remarried, and they've been together again for more than a decade. But not all wayward spouses respond to prayer. The founder of Covenant Keepers, who started the nonprofit in 1987 after her husband left her, is still "standing," the group's operations manager tells me. Naomi says she tells people whose mates don't respond that they'll still, somehow, be rewarded for keeping their marriage vows.

IT'S HARD to overstate the reach of the marriage-industrial complex. Even people who disdain it find themselves following its script. Julia, thirty-four, is a world away from Covenant Keepers, or any other group. She's a secular, politically liberal television producer who works in Manhattan and lives in a New Jersey suburb. She doesn't chat with strangers about her marriage, and she's never gone on a relationship retreat. Nevertheless, she has fully absorbed the values and even the narrative of the marriage-industrial complex.

I meet Julia at a sushi restaurant in New Jersey. She's the mother of an infant and a toddler. She's energetic, articulate, and rail thin. After we've spoken for a few minutes, I realize that she's been on the adultery diet. Soon after d-day, people stop eating. (When my husband heard this, he offered to have an affair if I ever start porking up.)

Julia began suspecting her husband when she noticed a pink envelope in the out-box of his home office, addressed to a female coworker. He said it was a friendship card; the woman was getting divorced because her husband had had an affair.

Julia mentioned this to some friends at work. "My guy friends were like, 'Guys don't send cards, especially not cards in a pink envelope, to someone they're friends with. He is sleeping with her.'" She dismissed this as ludicrous. But then she walked into her husband's home office and saw an e-mail on the screen that said "Kiss me" in giant letters. He said it was just flirting. "I said, 'I flirt with the best of them, but there's no circumstance where you write "Kiss me" to someone you have never kissed.'" Soon afterward Julia glanced at his screen again and saw an e-mail from the same woman, thanking him for taking her to a Broadway show in New York.

"So I flipped out, like, of course. I walked out of his office and into the living room, where he was sitting. And I was like, 'What the fuck is going on?'"

Her husband insisted again that they were just friends, but

Julia was apoplectic. She did what she figured anyone would do in her situation. "I said to him that night, 'You need to leave.'" Why did she decide this? "'Cause, I don't know, that's what you do, right? You find out something, and then they're supposed to leave. What was I going to say, 'Okay, good night,' and he'd come to bed?" Although kicking her husband out seemed like the only thing to do, it came straight from America's cultural script.

Julia's husband eventually moved back home, but he still wouldn't admit that he and the woman were more than good friends. Julia was in limbo. Everything pointed to an affair, but she didn't have proof. She feared that if she didn't know what was going on, she would get "walked on." "I began a personal crusade to find out every piece of information I could possibly get."

Julia went to a spy shop and got equipment to bug her husband's home office. At two every morning, while her kids were asleep upstairs and her husband was asleep on the spare bed in the basement, she snuck into the office and checked his e-mails and instant messages. Then she spent another few hours listening to all the phone conversations he'd had that day. "I mean, like, I didn't sleep for months. I was obsessed. I lost fifteen pounds, and, like, I don't have fifteen pounds. I was sick. I couldn't keep anything in. I was, like, shaking. I was a mess. And I was obsessed by the hunt." This quest for all the details of the affair is also, of course, straight from the playbook of the marriage-industrial complex.

Julia had a hunch that her husband had archived all of the

woman's past e-mails, but he had so many files for work on his computer that she couldn't find them. When he went to a funeral out of town, she resolved to go through every file in his computer. Eventually she hit the mother lode. The file was under the woman's maiden name. She had been drunk during their first sexual encounter and couldn't remember it, so over instant messages Julia's husband recounted the entire episode in detail. Julia also found descriptions of their meetings in different cities, when he was supposed to have been elsewhere on business trips. She had the flight itineraries. "I pieced together every single thing that had happened over the last year and a half between them," Julia says. "On the one hand, you're excited. On the other hand, I'm going to kill myself now." She printed everything out and had it waiting for him when he got home.

When she told her friends from work what she found, they said, "We told you, guys don't buy pink envelopes."

Although the wisdom of the marriage-industrial complex is ubiquitous, little of it has been tested. There's no empirical evidence that telling your spouse all the gory details of your affair helps him get over it or that couples are happier the more truthful they are. What if it's the opposite, and less truthfulness would make us happier? And what if we didn't treat adultery like a foreign invader that needs to be eradicated, but more like a fact of life? Would that take away some of the sting? I figure that if anyone knows how to deal with affairs, it's the French. So I start poking around in the city where I live: Paris.

death of the "five to seven"

I<small>T'S</small> <small>JANUARY</small> 1996. In the French village of Jarnac, where he was born seventy-nine years earlier, François Mitterrand lies in a closed oak casket. Looking on are his wife, Danielle, and their two sons. One step back is Anne Pingeot, the ex-president's longtime mistress. And standing alongside Danielle and her sons is Mazarine Pingeot, the twenty-one-year-old illegitimate daughter of Mitterrand and Anne.

Around the world this scene seemed to prove what everyone already knew about France: that *l'adultère* is a national pastime, that French wives tolerate their husbands' lovers (and may have a few of their own), and that having an affair is part of being a cultivated person in France, like eating foie gras. It was assumed that when the photo appeared in France's morning papers, not a single Parisian choked on his café crème.

When I moved from New York to Paris, many of my pre-conceptions about the French quickly proved true. Parisian women really are beautiful. I'm frequently humbled by waitresses who have such perfect skin they should be in L'Oréal advertisements. No one at the crowded public pools has cellulite, not even mothers with children. Pregnant women pop into little domes, then fit into their skinny jeans weeks after delivery. Parisians dress the part, too. No one goes grocery shopping in sweatpants, ever. People are realistic about the consequences for women who let themselves go. One forty-something mother of two sniffed to me that it's no wonder President Jacques Chirac is a bon vivant: His wife, Bernadette, always has a sour expression on her face.

Looking good makes it more fun to flirt. At dinner parties other women's husbands and boyfriends hold my gaze a bit longer than all but the most lecherous American men would dare. I never find out whether these approaches might lead to something more, but they don't have to. Flirting with someone else's partner isn't a betrayal of your spouse or a gateway to extramarital sex. It's a harmless way to have fun.

In France, fidelity seems like an idea you can play with, without sliding inexorably into sin. One of my French teachers suggests I polish my French in an *école horizontale*—that is, shacking up with a Frenchman for long enough to get my verb tenses straight. My husband nearly agrees that we can both do this, until I let it slip that I've already picked out my new "teacher."

Riding the Paris métro, I notice that French advertisers regularly joke about infidelity. A chain of movie theaters advertises its "fidelity card" for frequent customers with a billboard that declares, SUMMER'S OVER, BE FAITHFUL AGAIN. An optician's ad for a second pair of glasses shows a groom with a bride on each arm. In the buildup to Christmas, a chocolate company even speculates on how Santa himself keeps warm when he's out delivering presents; a commercial shows him in his sleigh accompanied by a fetching young woman who obviously isn't Mrs. Claus.

Evidence of the French love affair with adultery seems to be everywhere. Practically every romantic comedy I see is about married people and their lovers. And often no one dies! In one typical film, a couple takes their kids to the family house in southern France. Before long the wife's lover shows up for assignations on the beach and the father runs into a boyhood friend and realizes he's gay. By the end of the film, the husband and wife tearfully confess, move their lovers into the house with them, and, along with their children, sing a cheerful farewell to the audience. It's the reverse semiotics of most American movies, where having an affair means you're the villain. In the parlance of French films, cheating merely signifies that you're the protagonist.

In short, France looks like it's going to be a slam dunk for the book. I have moved into the world capital of infidelity, and I just need a few interviews with actual adulterers to round things out.

To my irritation, however, some parts of the story aren't falling into place. After I'm in Paris for a few months, one of the leading newsweeklies runs a cover story declaring the end of the taboo on adultery. This doesn't make sense, given my assumption that there hadn't been an adultery taboo to begin with. Even more perplexing is that the French actress featured in the story says she worked up the nerve to go public about her partner's infidelity only after seeing the American actress Uma Thurman do the same. "It's very American, one never sees this here," she explains.

I also notice that women's magazines are anything but blasé about affairs. Just as in America, they run stories on how to rein in cheating boyfriends and husbands, what to do if you suspect that your mate has strayed, how to get rid of a partner's threatening "best friend" of the opposite sex, and whether online sex counts as cheating. French women are startled when I tell them about their international reputation for being laissez-faire on infidelity. "Would you want your husband to cheat on you?" one woman replies.

And one by one my interviews evaporate. Friends of friends cancel appointments. E-mails aren't answered. People who initially seem titillated by the topic back off as soon as I take out my notepad. In Paris of all places, they are reluctant even to have anonymous conversations about it. When I complain about this to a friend and his French girlfriend, the young woman takes pity on me and suggests I'm running up against *pudeur,* a French word meaning something between modesty, privacy, and restraint. She offers to help. Then *she* stops returning my calls. If I hadn't lived in France, I might have left the country with empty notebooks. Surely if everyone in town is having *cinq à septs,* the famous "five to seven" o'clock rendezvous when they meet their lovers before heading home for dinner, a few would tell me about it?

And then I discover some statistics that defy all the stereotypes I had about France. It turns out that, in comparable sex surveys, French and American adults report almost identical rates of monogamy. Most French adults are boringly, staggeringly faithful. They pair up in their late twenties or early thirties and then spend the rest of their lives having trusty marital sex with the same partner, over and over again.

Alain Giami, who cowrote a paper comparing French and American sexual habits, says that not only are the French more faithful during courtship, but both French marriages and affairs last longer than they do in America. "In France, a relationship that has a sexual component appears to involve a higher degree of commitment than in the U.S.," Giami writes.

The American habit of juggling several suitors at once is foreign to most French people. If they've kissed, and certainly if they've slept together, French people tell me they assume they will be monogamous. "It's rare enough to meet someone that you're really attracted to," says a friend of mine, a French lawyer in her early thirties. "It would seem frivolous or careless" to court two people at once. She reminds me of the time she reluctantly agreed to be set up on a "blind date" with a friend of mine who was visiting from New York. The guy was nice, she says, but she found the "setup" format excruciating. "You cannot meet someone when the intention is to go further, *maybe*. It takes away the magic."

The more I dig, the more confusing things get. Opinion polls show that fidelity is the top quality French women seek in a mate, and that for men only a woman's "tenderness" rates slightly higher. Both genders say fidelity is second only to "dialogue" as the key to a couple's happiness. Given a choice, French people, like Americans, prefer to be faithful and believe that monogamy is the surest route to a successful relationship.

As I meet more people, I realize that the idea that French men set their mistresses up in small apartments sounds as quaint to the average Parisian as it would to someone in Cincinnati. It's just not practical. Forget the *cinq à sept*. The French upper middle classes—the ones supposedly enjoying the most affairs—are stuck at work until at least seven and then face a long trek home to the suburbs on the RER, Paris's version of the Long Island Rail Road. Real-estate prices have surged in the time I've lived here. When French yuppies are done buying nine-hundred-dollar imported strollers and paying off their ten-year mortgages, there isn't much left to keep a demanding mistress in a pied-à-terre, let alone find time to see her. Over lunch on the Champs-Elysées, a Parisian management consultant chuckles and tells me, "Sometimes when my wife and I have an argument, she says, 'I'm going to search for another man.' Afterward we laugh—no, our lives would be too complicated!"

Even the famous Mitterrand funeral photo turns out to be more complicated than it had seemed. Reading up in the French press, I learn that Mitterrand's "second family" had been kept a state secret for two decades. Though Mazarine's existence was known in political and journalism circles, it had been publicly disclosed only fourteen months before the funeral, when a photo of her and her father leaving a Paris restaurant ran on the cover of the weekly magazine *Paris-Match*.

Mitterrand was panicked about how the public would judge his second family. Soon after taking office in 1981, he formed a special antiterrorist squad that, though ostensibly charged with protecting the president, spent much of its time wiretapping political opponents and journalists who might name Anne and Mazarine or reveal other unpleasant truths about the president (including the fact that he had terminal cancer). The presidential palace apparently blocked publication of a book with details about Mazarine called *The Lost Honor of François Mitterrand* (it came out after he died). When Mitterrand's team learned that the author planned to discuss the manuscript on a live television show, the program was abruptly canceled. According to news reports, the government was so frightened of leaks that it bugged the author's local café and the home of the superintendent of his apartment building.

Years later, in her 2005 autobiography, *Mouth Sewn Shut,* Mazarine describes how she hid under the seat as she was driven from the presidential palace. In interviews she says she was so traumatized by the need to "stay invisible" that she went into psychotherapy. "I was born out of wedlock and hidden— the shame of the Republic, an affront to morality," she writes. Mitterrand, who had grown extremely close to Mazarine, added his name to her birth certificate toward the end of his life but stipulated that her official paternity shouldn't be disclosed until he died. Even the *Paris-Match* photos were said to be orchestrated by Mitterrand's team, to ease Mazarine carefully into public life.

What am I supposed to make of all this? France, my supposed slam dunk, is getting very complicated. The French don't fit the stereotypes about them. It's clear from the little I've seen that the rules about extramarital sex here are different from the ones in America. But unless I find people who'll tell me their stories, I fear that this country of 60 million people will remain an enigma.

MY FIRST STOP is at the home of Diane Johnson, a seventy-year-old American novelist who divides her time between Paris and San Francisco. She writes intricate comedies of manners set in France and almost always involving adultery. Though she is also a foreigner, I figure that from her perch on the border of these two cultures Johnson is well placed to untangle my confusion.

Johnson's Left Bank apartment is *haute bourgeois* Paris incarnate: molded stadium ceilings, books stacked on antique marble tables, and parquet floors that creak as she goes to fetch us coffee. Johnson's world, like those of her characters, is so hermetic that she admits it took her a while to realize not all French people have country houses. ("Though in my experience they do. Everyone I meet has a country house," she says.)

When we start talking about French adultery habits, how-ever, Johnson is stumped, too. "I don't actually know that much about the French rules, because it's hard to find out. If you're French, you know them, and if you're American there are certain things they won't tell you," she says. "What you hear, of course, is that French men have mistresses. . . . You wonder if it isn't part of a bygone or imagined France, the kind of thing that Colette writes about."

Colette is the early-twentieth-century French writer whose female characters moved in and out of relationships with bour-geois married men. The women sometimes wanted the money or other comforts that went with these arrangements, which made sense in a time when few women worked, upper-class marriages were still quasi-arranged, and divorce was taboo.

Nowadays, when practically everyone marries for love in France, the legacy of this era doesn't seem to be rampant adul-tery but rather the fact that French men delight in the company of women. Johnson describes her daily flirtations in the market, where it's "'just for you, madame, this lamb chop.' It makes the whole experience of going to the butcher something very nice and affirming for both parties," she says.

Johnson says married men in the milieu she frequents read fashion magazines, look at women's clothing in store windows, and accompany their wives on shopping expeditions. "French women will say that their mothers-in-law are terrible and irri-tating and control their sons, but the redux of that is that the sons are respectful."

By contrast, when she goes back to America, she observes

that gender relations there are confrontational and prone to hysterics. American men are sexually attracted to women but assume that women's habits are alien and prefer to watch sports with their buddies. "There's this model where the woman tries to get something out of the man and the man tries not to give it. Or vice versa. . . . There's an assumption that there's going to be disappointment and rancor and things have to be negotiated."

American women, she says, have been led down a "fulfill me" path in which "one of their big complaints was that their husbands wouldn't talk to them. But what they seemed to want to talk about was the relationship. . . . It's at once needy and boring." The implication is that modern French women might manage to avoid the unhelpful rounds of accusations and psychotherapy that accompany American affairs.

"French culture," Johnson says, dropping a lump of brown sugar into her espresso, "is sort of ourselves perfected."

I MEET UP with Charles at a smoky café near the Bastille that's filled with the kind of attractive, affluent young Parisians known as bourgeois bohemians, or "bobos." At forty-three, Charles is older than most of the people here. And though he's wearing a collarless white shirt and stylish black glasses, I sense he's at the bourgeois end of the bobo scale.

As he describes his life as a physician in Paris's well-off fifth arrondissement, across the Seine, Charles seems much like the urban professionals often depicted in French movies. He takes his three kids on sailing vacations. He plays the violin in an amateur orchestra. He met his wife of fifteen years, who's also a doctor, when both were medical interns. He has the occasional religious moment but considers himself agnostic.

Although we've met to discuss Charles's extramarital affairs, he starts out by stressing that he went into his marriage intending to be faithful for life and was monogamous for the first decade. He would have continued that way if his wife had kept up her side of the marital bargain. She was loving, affectionate, and a good mother, but she made no effort to be sexy. Charles begged her to wear high heels and skirts that showed off her great figure. Instead, despite years of pleading, she wore baggy clothes and left the house without even putting on lipstick. Her interest in actually having sex was negligible.

It was nice that she was intelligent. But Charles craved a woman who was "feminine." Surely that wasn't too much for a man to expect, especially a self-described romantic like Charles. But she didn't comply. After a decade of this, and despite the fact that he was raised to believe that marriage equaled monogamy, Charles felt he had no choice but to see other women.

Unlike in America, there are practically ironclad reasons to have affairs here. "I don't feel very much guilt, because I asked her so many times to change, to dress more nicely, more sexy, to go to the hairstylist," he says.

One night, at a bar near his house, he met a married woman who actually was a hairstylist. Charles describes the woman, Danielle, with obvious admiration: she's blond, fabulously sexual, and goes to the gym daily. She's so concerned about her looks that when she got breast implants, she refused even to see Charles until the swelling went down.

At first it was very romantic, and they exchanged lots of presents. (At the peak of his infatuation, he gave her a Gucci watch.) Now, five years later, it's more of an amorous friendship. They meet for lunch on Fridays, when Charles works half days, at the same restaurant near the Odéon métro. Then they make love at the studio next to Charles's family apartment.

"This is not what I expected from my life. Probably [fidelity] is still the best situation, but it's not possible with my wife. I have to make compromises. I had to adapt." Because of his children, the oldest of whom is twelve, he wouldn't consider divorce.

Charles tries to be discreet. When his wife caught him walking Danielle to the métro a few years back, he pacified her by claiming it was just a onetime drunken fling. The conversation was over by the time they went to sleep, though she occasionally brings it up again when they argue. (They refer to the incident as Charles's "mistake.") If she suspects there's more going on, she doesn't mention it.

I can't help thinking that in America, Charles would be called a narcissist, a sexual addict, or worse. But he and his peers view his relationship with Danielle in pragmatic rather than moral terms: In his situation he sees no way of being both a contented person and a faithful husband. "I warned her many times. I said, 'If you don't give me what I want, I will seek it somewhere else.' But she didn't understand. I did my best for ten years working on it, but trying to change it didn't work."

Given that, he doesn't punish himself over the affair. The few friends he's told about Danielle don't judge him either. He's not at all ashamed of his arrangement, but he rarely mentions it, because he wants to make sure his wife never finds out. Why spoil a good thing or add rancor to his marriage?

When I tell Charles that Americans often go into psychotherapy to manage the stress of leading a double life like his, he looks confused. About a year after beginning the affair with Danielle, he finally left the therapist he'd been seeing for six years. "I solved the problems," he explains. "The problems were marriage and sex."

I LEAVE MY meeting with Charles feeling giddy. I'm finally peering behind the curtains. I already know there isn't much difference between how many affairs people in France and America have, but there seem to be big differences in the inner lives of the people who have them, and in the way others treat them.

The most striking thing about my conversation with Charles is what he doesn't say: that people in romantic relationships should be completely honest with each other. Lying to his wife didn't bother him, and no one he knows in France (besides me) has suggested it should.

It reminds me of what the *New Yorker*'s Adam Gopnik wrote during the Clinton trials: "The real difference—which is much harder for Americans to accept—is not that the French are less excitable about sex. It's that they're a lot calmer about lies."

When I trot out the American maxim that "it's not about the sex, it's about the lying," French people just look confused. How exactly could you have an affair without lying about it? they wonder. They are perplexed by the nearly religious zeal with which Americans believe that couples shouldn't keep secrets. Philosophical disagreements aside, it just doesn't seem practical to them.

"The arresting—and perhaps instructive—French attitude seems to be that lying about sex is merely another of the social graces," writes Gopnik. He goes on to say that "In France, the unshocked assumption that ordinary people—politicians, lovers, journalists—lie a lot means that you can talk about lies, and punish them appropriately, without turning every lie into a capital offense."

Discretion seems to be the cornerstone of adultery in France. But unlike Americans, French people aren't quiet about their affairs because they're ashamed of their behavior. Rather, most don't want to spoil a good thing by opening the door to gossip. And because affairs last longer in France, keeping things quiet becomes even more important.

"They're not uncomfortable; they [just] don't want to have troubles," explains Alain Giami, who co-authored the French-American sex study. "There are dark sides of the relationship that are not shared."

And since lying isn't the real problem, then confession isn't the cure. The author of a French self-help book on fidelity says there's wisdom behind the French maxim "It's not good to speak all truths." The idea of someone's bursting out with a confession of adultery, because she just couldn't live with herself otherwise, seems like the stuff of Hollywood movies.

In fact, some French affairs can seem like Cold War conflicts in which neither side ever draws its guns. Franck, forty-seven, a manager at a Paris computer company, realized his wife had a lover when he had to refill the gas in their car much more often than before. When she denied that anything was going on, he began seeing one of his coworkers. A few months later, when his wife said she wanted to accept a job in Lyon, "my interpretation was that she wanted to put an end to her own affair," Franck says.

He was wrong. She moved to Lyon ahead of him, and when he called her office one day, he found out she was on an overnight business trip to Paris but hadn't contacted him there. So he upped the ante and had a fling with her best friend.

Franck finally figured out that his wife's affair had petered off when "after a few months she was still going to Paris for work, but she stopped staying overnight." He moved to Lyon, and their marriage improved without a direct conversation about what had transpired. Franck suspects that her affair was with one of his good friends but says, "somehow I didn't feel like forcing it." It was, he says, "maybe enough for me to know when it ended."

He accepts that she felt a loyalty to her lover and may have promised never to disclose the details, just as he had promised the same to her best friend. "I think she fell in love, really, with someone else. Otherwise nothing would make sense," he says. He no longer worries about it and is pleased that lately they've been quite close. "It was a problem mainly if she decided to leave," he says.

It's hard for me to believe that Franck is satisfied knowing so little, but Giami, the French researcher, says Franck's story is typical. "It's like people don't want to know. It's not explicit, but it's not implicit. It's not confessed. People will not say, 'I have a lover.' The partner feels that there is something else or someone else but doesn't want to know more about it," he says.

Véronique, a Parisian high-school teacher in her forties, explains it to me this way: "To respect the partner, it means not to try to look for everything you'd like to know, to accept what he said and not to try to look for information he doesn't want to give you."

I am also struck that most people I interview aren't tortured and conscience-racked about their own affairs. Guilt doesn't seem to feature very heavily in the adultery script here. They don't think extramarital sex points to larger moral failings or that it has transformed them into "sinners." They view adultery as a transgression, but one that's forgivable and even understandable. Both Franck and Charles are satisfied that they have weighed their options and made good decisions. Practically no one they know has suggested otherwise. Indeed, once the initial barrier to cheating was breached, they saw no reason not to enjoy themselves. Why ruin it by being neurotic?

Even the people I meet who disapprove of infidelity (and

polls show there are many) are reluctant to preach. They tell me that other people's behavior, while interesting as gossip, is ultimately their own business. That's in stark contrast to America, where adulterers frequently make the bizarre claim that they aren't the sort of people who would have affairs, presumably because they can't reconcile their behavior with their need to believe they're good people. Even Americans who make a strong intellectual case for infidelity sounded defensive. That's because, unlike people in France, they are contending with an underlying social message—coming from the movies, their families, their friends—that infidelity is wrong and that adulterers are sinners.

Religion partly accounts for these differences. Although most French people identify as Catholic and may even have been baptized, just 11 percent say religion is "very important" to them, compared to 59 percent of Americans. France is now one of the least religious countries in Europe, especially among people under fifty. The implication for adultery is that, for the French, fidelity isn't an a priori rule endorsed by God; it's just a good idea. But, like all good ideas, there are circumstances when it doesn't quite apply.

Monogamy is still the optimal state. Practically all those I spoke to said they'd prefer to be faithful. But when infidelity happens, the French don't seem to panic and assume that cheating will endanger society or that it will spill over into people's job performances. They view it as a self-contained act, not a slippery slope into moral depravity. One woman in her twenties tells me that after she and her married boyfriend came out of the closet and slow-danced at their office Christmas party, at a French public-relations firm, coworkers congratulated them. It was obvious they were in love, she says, and romance gets respect.

We Americans aren't reluctant moralizers at all, and with good reason. In one pervasive version of the American adultery story, affairs left unchecked eventually poison one's whole life. That explains "codes of conduct" in universities and offices. If corporate executives can cheat on their spouses, the thinking sometimes goes, they're surely capable of embezzlement and accounting fraud, too. And because infidelity is a social crime, American philanderers are expected to show remorse to friends, employees, constituents, fans, and anyone else they've "duped." But the only person Charles ever expects to apologize to is his wife. If it never comes to that, all the better.

ARE THE FRENCH really ourselves perfected? Does accepting that affairs are a fact of life rather than a shocking aberration make French people happier or better off? I pose this question to Aurélie, a modern-day *femme mondaine* whose very existence seems calculated to make me feel naïve and overweight. Aurélie, thirty-six, has long legs and long brown hair. She speaks a delicately accented but otherwise perfect English and punctuates her carefully constructed arguments with a confident twitch of the head. I can't imagine her eating at McDonald's or watching a *Star Wars* sequel. She lives in a converted artist's loft that's filled with books, several of which she's written (my hunch is she decided to speak to me out of writerly solidarity).

Aurélie attended the same high school as Mitterrand's daughter, Mazarine, and said all the students knew who Mazarine's father was, though of course no one said anything about it to Mazarine. "I would never judge anyone's decision in their private life, unless they're preventing someone's freedom," Aurélie explains.

Aurélie, who's divorced, is now part of the Parisian intellectual elite. She consults with the government on gender issues and goes to dinner parties where thin women and their handsome husbands debate "positive discrimination" and drop in-the-know comments about politicians' private lives. One of the pleasures of these evenings, Aurélie says, is knowing that you had an afternoon tryst with the man across the table, who's now passing the cheese plate to his wife.

"It's all very French," she tells me, looking up for a reaction. Extramarital sex becomes "adultery" only when your partner finds out, she says. "When it happened to me, I did not think of it as something within my marriage. I did not hesitate, I did not say no. It just happened," she says. "With me and my circle of friends, the only space where you could call it adultery is where you deal with your husband's feelings. . . . If you only look at the relationship between me and my lover, there's no adultery. There's just us."

I tell Aurélie that Americans often believe they've sinned

even if no one else ever finds out. For religious people it's as if God is in the motel room with them. Even nonbelievers have attacks of conscience that feel a lot like religious guilt.

I might as well have declared my devotion to processed cheese. Secularism is another mark of French sophistication. "There is no God in France. It's over. His career is over," Aurélie says with a wave of her hand. "The only moral thing that's important in this adultery thing is trying to spare people's feelings."

Increasingly, infidelity in France isn't even extramarital. As elsewhere in Europe, the French are choosing cohabitation over marriage. In 1999, France began issuing civil partnerships known as PACS (*pacte civil de solidarité*), for both gay and straight people. PACS offer some of the legal and financial benefits of marriage, but either party can dissolve one with three months' notice.

Of course, there are plenty of French people who have passionate love affairs and leave their partners for their lovers. But in a casual affair, even a heated one, it's common to limit the level of emotional involvement, or at least the level of emotional rhetoric, out of respect for your partner at home. "Nobody ever says 'I love you' in that kind of story, in text messages or e-mail. You say 'I miss you.' You say 'I love you' to only one person, and that's the one who's waiting for you at home," Aurélie tells me. She searches for a name for this kind of relationship and decides on "liaison."

I get the sense that this nonchalance about extramarital sex doesn't come entirely naturally. Aurélie and others of her generation keep stressing how *French* their attitudes are, as if "Frenchness" were something they've achieved through careful study and practice.

The French press does this, too. French newspapers famously sneered at the American media frenzy that surrounded the Clinton-Lewinsky scandal. When *Paris-Match* published the photos of Mitterrand and his daughter, a writer in the highbrow daily *Le Monde* chided the magazine for forgetting the rules of Frenchness, saying, "The 'secrets' of the private life of political men merit interest on the condition that one replies affirmatively to two questions: Do they reveal a misleading practice that contradicts the public discourse of the person concerned? Do they influence the exercise of his duties?"

It took a while to see that these sneers were calculated to make outsiders, both French and American, feel like the cloddish woman in the parlor who blushes at a racy story. But even the establishment papers sometimes couldn't keep up their cosmopolitan façades. When Monicagate was in full gear, *Le Monde* rushed to press with an eighteen-thousand-word French translation of the Starr Report, accompanied by biographical sketches of all the characters involved. For bilingual readers it posted the entire English version on its Web site.

Another self-conscious mark of Frenchness is to deconstruct the idea of fidelity until it practically falls apart. Never mind that every couple marrying in France must vow "fidelity, aid and assistance" at their town hall. In the hands of astute Parisians, this seemingly airtight promise isn't binding. Practically every educated French person I interviewed began our conversation with an exegesis of what "fidelity" really means.

"'Fidelity' is fidelity to what?" asks Véronique, the Parisian teacher. She says her decision to be monogamous with her former husband was simply a pragmatic choice. Véronique says that a colleague's husband recently left her for another woman. Véronique's analysis is that if he had stayed with his wife, he wouldn't truly be faithful, since his heart would be with someone else. "The first infidelity is this infidelity: Can you be faithful to what you are?" Véronique says. Others tell me that "fidelity" is an important value but that it has more to do with love than with sex.

This hyperintellectualization of adultery can fall apart, too. About a year after our first meeting, even Aurélie's carefully constructed veneer fractures. She tells me she's now embroiled in a full-blown infidelity *scandale.* Her latest lover, a man she met through work, is preparing to leave his girlfriend and two children. Aurélie is pleased. But she's extremely nervous about the kids and about her new, more official role in the man's life. There's been a lot of emotional upheaval. "I'm not so sure about this adultery thing anymore," she keeps saying.

Indeed, the ethics of *l'adultère* get trickier as they approach one's own life. "Socially tolerated, individually unbearable" is how the newsweekly *L'Express* describes it. Adultery "embodies the expression of liberty, but it can bring about a radical reaction on the part of the person who suffers from it." This means that while people aren't amazed to discover that their partner has cheated on them, they're still devastated.

Even in the emotional realm, there are differences between French and Americans, however. Most Americans who discover a partner's affair become determined to get back into a monogamous situation, either with the same person or someone new. Couples therapy, long conversations, and even divorce are all meant to restore monogamy. Americans don't lose their faith in fidelity even after fidelity fails them in practice.

In France, however, the "victims" of cheating emerge less starry-eyed from their ordeals. Since fidelity is viewed as a good idea rather than a God-given necessity, the experience sometimes convinces them that fidelity just isn't possible. The French newsweekly *Le Nouvel Observateur* quotes a forty-year-old aesthetician who leaves her partner after catching him on the street with another woman. Instead of looking for a new man who'll be faithful, as she might in the American version of this story, she finds a new partner who is married. "At least when he cheats on me, I know who he's doing it with," she says.

I KEEP HEARING about a "young philosopher" who's writing a treatise on infidelity. I'm eager to meet her, but other academics warn me that she's a "conservative" and that I should be wary.

I'm ready for a right-wing firebrand when the petite, thirty-five-year-old Michela Marzano opens the door to her apartment. As we sit down for coffee amid airy modern furniture, I keep waiting for the blow that doesn't come. By American standards Marzano sounds mainstream, even boring. Her argument is essentially that partners should be sexually faithful to each other and that the lying that accompanies infidelity harms a relationship.

But apparently, to French academics, this argument sounds religious, paternalistic, and outdated. It's one thing to believe privately in fidelity, but it's quite another to suggest—as Marzano does in her book *Fidelity: Loving on the Edge*—that others should believe in it, too.

Marzano is Italian, but she writes in French and has made her intellectual home at Paris's National Center of Scientific Research. She knows what she's up against. "There's not only a refusal of religion; there's a sort of refusal of morality," she complains. France's establishment doesn't want to accept that "there are some values that are very important to people," including fidelity. She says French people now in their forties prize personal freedom. But the free choices they make, including getting divorced, aren't making them happy. Having witnessed this, people in their twenties are more romantic and find fidelity appealing, she says.

Marzano says humans are happier when they accept boundaries, even though boundaries limit their behavior and oblige them to give up some short-term pleasures, such as extramarital sex. "What I wanted to show is that Don Juan is not free; because he's completely a slave of his drives, he's not able to construct his life," she says. "Probably you are more free if you accept some restraints."

And what if monogamy doesn't make you happy either? "It's true that one person will never be enough," she says. "But people aren't something you use to fill a hole inside of you. They are not objects."

THE ONLY REALM of French life where infidelity is truly de rigueur is politics. Indeed, the fact that a powerful man has a mistress doesn't in itself qualify as news, simply because there's nothing new in it. In fact, French voters are drawn to candidates who seem like they can attract lots of women. "Politicians are seducers, that's part of their job. They're salespeople also," Franck, the computer programmer, tells me. One tell-all book, *Sexus Politicus,* suggests that socialist Lionel Jospin never made the leap from prime minister to president because he wasn't sufficiently seductive. The French certainly like to keep tabs on who their leaders are bedding. There was a flurry of interest in 2003 when a government regulator was investigated for allegedly organizing sadomasochistic parties with prostitutes. Several books by prominent journalists, detailing the peccadilloes of politicians and their lovers, down to what they ordered from room service, have briefly been the talk of Paris. But interest in a politician's private affairs has more to do with gossip than scandal. The unsubstantiated rumor that Jacques Chirac has a Japanese son (how else to explain his dozens of trips there?) was recounted to me by people eager to prove they were part of the cognoscenti, not to show they disapproved of his behavior.

The French press, which also has to contend with strict privacy laws, gets worked up only when a story deviates from the standard infidelity script or when it contains very juicy details about a particular case. The result is that the infidelity stories that run in the French media aren't typical cases; they're published precisely because they can surprise a French audience. These stories aren't offered up as morality tales or told as if a public hero has disappointed the nation's children. There's certainly no suggestion that a politician's job performance will suffer. The subject has merely been caught in an unusual, and therefore newsworthy, situation.

Mitterrand's story was worth exposing in *Paris-Match* not because he had extramarital sex but because he had a whole extramarital family. According to reports after his death, while he was president, Mitterrand spent at least as many nights with his mistress, Anne Pingeot, a curator at the Musée d'Orsay, as he did with his wife. He installed Anne and Mazarine in a government apartment and used state security services to protect them. Pingeot was more of a second wife, something that's off script even for French presidents.

In the summer of 2005, the French media took an interest in another off-script story: the marital troubles of Nicolas and Cécilia Sarkozy. Though the Sarkozys surely weren't the only political couple with a stormy marriage, certain elements of their story made it worth reporting.

Nicolas Sarkozy, fifty, is a former protégé of Jacques Chirac. As a twenty-five-year-old party worker, he spun what was supposed to be a five-minute address to the party congress into a rousing twenty-minute oratory that made him a rising political star. The stocky, dark-haired son of a Hungarian immigrant,

"Sarko" has led various ministries and makes no secret of wanting to be president. His straightforward manner and obvious ambition have earned him the reputation for being an "American-style" politician.

In 1996 he married his second wife Cécilia, forty-eight, a former model and daughter of a Russian émigré father and a Spanish mother. The tall and glamorous Cécilia emerged as Sarkozy's main adviser and constant companion. As Sarkozy's star rose, he made no secret of his dependence on the counsel of his wife, who had her own office next door to his. A government adviser who went to meetings with them told me Sarkozy watched Cécilia's face for approval as he spoke. Their marriage became part of his public image. He took the unusual step of posing for *Paris-Match* on his morning jog with Cécilia, and with their young son, Louis, kicking a soccer ball around. These photo shoots buffered charges that the couple was "à la Kennedy."

Since Sarkozy had made his married life public, some French media felt it was fair game to point out, in May 2005, that Cécilia was no longer ubiquitous at his side. Sarkozy admitted to a French TV interviewer that the couple was working through some issues. Rumors swirled that Cécilia was having an affair, and then a relative confirmed that the pair had separated. Then, in August 2005, *Paris-Match* published photographs of Cécilia accompanied by Richard Attias, forty-nine, the head of a French event-planning company who had directed Sarkozy's "coronation" as party chief. In one of the *Paris-Match* photos, Attias and Cécilia are on Manhattan's Upper East Side studying what appears to be the layout plan for an apartment. In another they're holding hands at an outdoor table at L'Esplanade in central Paris, a hangout for journalists and politicians near the National Assembly. It's a very public place, where people go when they have something to signal. The headline reads "Cécilia Sarkozy: The Hour of Choice."

Cécilia was way off script. What sort of political wife jumps ship just before her husband has a real shot at the presidency? And why was she flaunting her new relationship at L'Esplanade? Was she really willing to sacrifice her chance to be First Lady for what appeared to be love? Paris was abuzz. Could the whole affair be a grand publicity stunt?

A cuckolded and possibly abandoned husband was off script, too. A week after the *Paris-Match* photos appeared, another weekly ran pictures of a sad-looking Nicolas with the headline "Broken by his marital crisis." Reports claimed that he had lost weight.

Most of the coverage didn't even bother mentioning the adultery-filled backstory of the Sarkozys' marriage, which was whispered about among the cognoscenti. According to this gossip, Sarkozy fell for Cécilia in 1984, when he officiated at her marriage to her first husband, Jacques Martin, a television host. At the time Sarkozy was mayor of the upscale Paris suburb Neuilly-sur-Seine and was married to his first wife, with whom he has two grown children.

Sarkozy apparently didn't become magically monogamous after he married Cécilia either. "Everyone knows he was having many affairs himself," the government adviser told me. The difference is that "all the other wives—Mrs. Chirac, Mrs. Mitterrand, Mrs. Giscard d'Estaing—their husbands had affairs and they stayed." One of Sarkozy's previous conquests was rumored to be Jacques Chirac's younger daughter, another source of tension between the two political rivals.

According to the whispers in Paris, Cécilia fell for Attias after she clashed with Sarkozy's other advisers over his presidential strategy. *Le Nouvel Observateur* later reported that just as Cécilia was feeling politically marginalized, an anonymous letter arrived listing the "dates, names and places" of Sarkozy's extramarital conquests. "In normal times Cécilia without a doubt would have thrown the letter in the trash," and considered it a ploy against her husband, the magazine said. Instead it apparently fueled her discontent. Shortly afterward she told an interviewer that she doesn't fit into the "mold" of First Lady. "I'm not politically correct. I walk around in jeans, cargo pants and cowboy boots," she said. She soon left Paris to meet Attias at a conference he had organized in Petra, Jordan, where Bill Clinton was among the attendees, and then followed Attias to New York.

Back in Paris, Sarkozy set about trying to make Cécilia jealous. He apparently took up with an attractive journalist from the newspaper *Le Figaro,* who had published a critical biography of Jacques Chirac. The two were seen grocery shopping together, and Sarkozy introduced her to his inner circle of friends.

But this was just a side story, perhaps because it was so predictable. The real drama for the French media was Cécilia's unexpected life choice. None of the French papers moralized about the Sarkozys' mutual philandering. Indeed, instead of issuing an American-style apology, Sarkozy told the press to back off and had a French publisher pulp a pending biography of his wife that was appropriately called *Cécilia Sarkozy: Between Heart and Reason.* He reportedly threatened to sue a French newspaper that published the name of the *Figaro* journalist. The editor of *Paris-Match* was forced to resign over the photos of Cécilia and Attias.

By January the French public learned that the Sarkozys had reconciled when the couple made a fifteen-minute appearance together at L'Esplanade, where television cameras were waiting. By late summer the two were posing arm in arm on a beach in Cyprus. *Gala,* another French glossy, ran photos of them lounging beneath a tree in Morocco under the headline "Summer of Pardon." A story inside explained how Sarkozy had flown "incognito" to New York to convince Cécilia to come back to him. *Le Nouvel Observateur* speculated that Cécilia's departure had been the result of a "delayed crisis of adolescence." This happy ending put the Sarkozys back on script as just another political couple who, it's presumed, may occasionally cheat on each other again.

The sexual script that Cécilia Sarkozy originally broke from was followed almost to the letter by First Lady Bernadette Chirac, wife of French president Jacques Chirac. Bernadette comes from a more aristocratic family than Cécilia Sarkozy does, and, at seventy-three, she's practically two generations older. But in a sign that even the aristocracy is changing, we know Bernadette's views on extramarital sex from her own memoirs.

In the fall of 2001, a year before the presidential elections in which Chirac would seek a second term, his former chauffeur published a tell-all detailing the president's affairs with party workers, actresses, and secretaries. According to the chauffeur, whom Chirac had recently fired, the president was known for the sheer speed of his trysts ("three minutes, with the shower *après* included," members of his staff joked). The chauffeur wrote that Chirac apparently envied Mitterrand's outsize sexual reputation and set out to bed any woman the dead president had also seduced. Bernadette, the chauffeur wrote, was a jealous woman who waited at the window for her husband to come home.

Chirac's handlers were apparently concerned that allowing a chauffeur to color the president's private life would damage the campaign, and they wanted to win over the far right with Bernadette's religiosity and her opposition to abortion. So, shortly before the chauffeur's book was released, France's First Lady published *Conversation,* a 228-page extended interview. In it Bernadette admits that her husband's unfaithfulness pained her and that she considered leaving him over it. But, in a uniquely French act of political spin, she doesn't exactly blame him for playing the field. "He's a handsome man, and also very seductive, very lively. So the girls, they go wild for that. . . . But yes, of course I was jealous. . . . The luck of my husband is that I was a very reasonable girl, I believe. But I was jealous sometimes. Very! He was a very handsome boy. And he also had the magic of words. Women are very sensitive to that. . . . One finds this in all the professions. A great surgeon, a great doctor, a minister. It's human. But one still must resist."

She, too, painted infidelity as one of the normal problems in a lengthy relationship. "Life is not a long tranquil river," she says. "Yet, when one decides to build a house together, I believe that the result is unshakable. In my opinion, that's the beauty of marriage.

"The convention holds that in this type of situation one puts forth a façade and one suffers the blows. . . . As for my in-laws, my mother-in-law told me when I got married, 'Above all no divorce in this family.'"

Though *Conversation* was published four years before L'Affaire Sarkozy, it seems aimed at women like Cécilia. "Lately there's something that ruffles me. It's the number of married women who meet another man in their workplace. Suddenly, the husband has all the defects in the world and voilà, good-bye, they leave. . . . I find this an extraordinary phenomenon. Again, I'm not making a value judgment, it's just an observation.

"You have to find the courage to say, 'There are bad periods.' What life doesn't have them? . . . In any case, I've often warned [Chirac], 'The day that Napoleon abandoned Josephine, he lost everything.'"

Despite her plug for traditional values, Bernadette's confessional succeeded in winning the modern media game. *Conversation* sold two hundred thousand copies in its first month. The book's publisher explained to *Le Monde* that "what's interesting are the books by the inner circle, in the corridors, the ones that go behind the scenes." And President Chirac, of course, won a second term.

There's something true about the foreigners' cliché that says Frenchmen like Chirac have a lightness about adultery, that they see it as one of life's pleasures, like crème brûlée. When the French have affairs, they do a better job of enjoying them than Americans do. And they don't pursue the American ideal of total truth within marriage.

But, in another sense, most French people don't live up to their stereotype. It turns out that the vast majority of them—the ones who are not presidents—do believe in fidelity. They don't commit rampant adultery. However, there is a country not too far away where a large swath of the population does exactly that and doesn't feel at all guilty about it. It's called Russia.

the obligatory affair

I'M SO USED to French people backing off when I mention extramarital affairs that when I arrive in Moscow, I'm reluctant to broach the topic directly. Instead, during an interview with a family psychologist on one of my first days there, I start out by saying I'm researching "marriage" and only gradually admit I'm most interested in affairs.

I quickly realize that my bashfulness is wasted. The psychologist perks up at the mere mention of infidelity.

"Nowadays it's a must, that type of relationship. It's obligatory," she says with a sudden authoritative air.

Is she joking? I'm sure we must have misunderstood each other, so through the interpreter I ask whether she means *extramarital affairs* are obligatory?

The psychologist doesn't flinch. "I think it's wise," she says. To prove her point, she tells me she herself has enjoyed a number of extramarital affairs throughout her own fifteen-year marriage, though lately work obligations have caused her to cut back. She asks that I please quote her full name—Svetlana Artemova—which she writes in my notebook to make sure I get the spelling right.

I've heard therapists say affairs can strengthen a relationship, but I've never heard one insist that extramarital sex is an essential ingredient of a happy marriage; that affairs are *obligatory*. Could this be the fringe view of one Russian shrink? My interpreter, Anna, insists that Artemova is a respected psychologist with a thriving practice. Anna, who's divorced with a grown son herself, adds that she agrees with Artemova's assessment and doesn't find it surprising.

MOSCOW LOOKS like a stage set for all kinds of transgressions. First there's the film-noir lighting. In November, it's already so dark that my camera flash goes off in the middle of the day. Nighttime is even eerier: Kiosks selling every kind of liquor provide the only illumination on residential streets.

After just a day or two of traveling around to interviews, I get the creepy feeling that lots of people are on the make, even for small amounts of money. I don't doubt that as a foreigner I'm an easy target. But I've never seen such remorseless opportunism. The women who sell tickets for the metro routinely shortchange me, then just shrug and hand over the difference when I make a fuss. An official taxi driver tells me it will cost fifteen dollars to get to my hotel, then refuses to renegotiate and holds my luggage hostage in his trunk when the hotel turns out to be four blocks away.

Everyone's an entrepreneur. To hail an unofficial taxi, I just raise my arm and ordinary drivers stop to negotiate a rate. It's best to buckle up, however. The traffic is so menacing that pedestrians run across big intersections even when they have the right of way. Sidewalks aren't much safer. Groups of drunken young men amble around at night, and in the mornings I pass men with fresh wounds on their faces, probably from brawls or inebriated falls the night before. I gawk, but no one else looks twice.

There's a good reason for the desperate mood. Most Muscovites earn the equivalent of just a few hundred dollars a month, and yet Moscow is so expensive I opt to stay in a youth hostel. Drink is a big killer, and so is a general unhealthiness. A friend who worked for a law firm in Moscow tells me the receptionist kept a heart-attack kit in her desk. And then there are the dangers from outside: An Englishman tells me that soon after he arrived, his landlord stopped by to offer him "protection."

Moscow has a new middle class, but only a sliver of the population is part of it. Medical doctors and university professors tell me they're not "middle class," since they can't afford to buy a car or eat in restaurants, and they live in small apartments with their spouses, kids, and in-laws. And they don't expect their circumstances to improve, the way they might in America. As in Soviet times, most people in the "new Russia" will live in the same apartment for their entire adult lives.

Against this bleak backdrop, it's not surprising that Russians have some extramarital affairs to cheer themselves up. But I'm still shocked that they have so many of them. There's never been a reliable sex study of the whole nation, but that 1996 poll in St. Petersburg found that about half of men and about a quarter of women had had an affair during their current marriage. This means the lifetime level of affairs—which would include past marriages, too—is even higher. Urban Russians seem to be more adulterous than people anyplace else in the industrialized world.

Or at least they claim to be. The social sanction on affairs is so weak in Russia that I have a hunch men who don't cheat might say they do, to make themselves look good. In an attitudes survey done in 1994, nearly 40 percent of Russians said affairs are "not at all" wrong or "only sometimes" wrong—compared to 6 percent of Americans answering similarly. In fact, Russians approved of infidelity more than people in any of the two dozen countries in the study did. It's the first place I've visited where people boast about being unfaithful.

Is all this cheating, real or imagined, a problem for Russians? Would they be better off if they didn't jump in the sack with their neighbors' wives? I've arrived at the industrial world's presumed epicenter of extramarital sex to find out why Russians commit so much adultery and whether it works for them.

WHEN I ASK about sex in Soviet times, Russians almost always recite the national joke: "There was no sex in the Soviet Union." In the 1930s and '40s, Stalin's government banned sex education and made it practically impossible for anyone, even gynecologists, to get books on the topic. Officials prohibited virtually any public discussion of sex and wouldn't let scientists research it. Schools taught the virtues of chaste friendship and urged citizens to channel their sexual energy into building the state. Sexologist Igor Kon says the government was threatened by sex because it was one of the few realms out of its control. "What poses a danger to totalitarianism is not so much elementary physiological sex as individual passionate love," Kon writes in his book *The Sexual Revolution in Russia.*

Of course, there was a big gap between the official rhetoric and the way people really behaved. High-ranking Communists spent state funds maintaining their lovers, procuring banned Western pornography, and hosting the occasional orgy. A culture minister who served under Nikita Khrushchev was caught keeping a harem of young actresses. When the future Soviet leader Leonid Brezhnev was posted to Kazakhstan earlier in his career, he apparently took several mistresses with him.

By the 1960s anyone who suspected a spouse of cheating could turn him or her in to the local Communist party boss. The party would convene a meeting, and anyone found "guilty" of adultery could be kicked out of the party and lose any chance of ever getting a better job. Party officials tolerated some scientific discussion of sex, depending on their moods. Kon recalls that when one of his graduate students sought approval to do a poll on youth sexual behavior, the local party chief forbade him to include the question "How many sexual partners have you had?" The chief asked, "What does that mean? Personally, I'm living with my wife," Kon says, though it was common knowledge that the man was also "personally living with a number of ballet dancers from the Kirov Theater."

There were many practical impediments to cheating. Adulterous women risked getting pregnant and having to suffer through an abortion, which was the main form of birth control. But older people tell me the biggest problem was simply finding a place to meet their lovers. Unmarried people weren't allowed to rent hotel rooms, particularly not in their own cities, and police patrolled public parks. Home was out of the question: In addition to children and in-laws, many people lived in communal apartments where they shared kitchens and bathrooms with other families. "We are born in the hallway, we make love in the hallway, and we die in the hallway," a sculptor in Moscow told the writer Mark Popovsky in the 1970s.

And yet, Russians went to great lengths to enjoy a bit of freedom from the party's near-total control, and from the drudgery of daily life. The Moscow–St. Petersburg express train was dubbed "the hotel on wheels" because couples could rent private carriages. Friends borrowed keys to one another's apartments. Marina, a sixty-four-year-old dentist who lives in Moscow, doesn't seem like much of a dissident. She still pines for the job security she had in Soviet times. But in the 1980s she had a multiyear affair with a KGB agent, risking both of their jobs and marriages. They would often meet in the apartment of one of Marina's close friends, who was usually away during the day.

Why did she risk it?

"Maybe because it was such a bad offense," she tells me.

Also, other people she knew were doing the same thing. She'd run into them with their lovers at the informal lounges where artists gathered, which were considered safe spots. "I knew about many people really, but it wasn't discussed too much," she says. "You see, the word 'sex' sounded like prostitution. But the idea of sex was very widespread."

Artyom Troitsky, editor of *Playboy*'s Russian edition, puts this idea more precisely. "Sex was the last thing they couldn't take away from us, and that's why we did it so much. Everyone had affairs with everyone. Moscow was the most erotic city in the world," he told Derk Sauer, a Dutch media magnate and columnist who lives in Moscow.

Soviet citizens were also used to lying. "We pretend to work, and they pretend to pay us," was the unofficial slogan. Lies were so important for survival that they came to seem like a good thing, without any moral baggage. The sexologist Sergei Agarkov, also quoted by Sauer, explains, "We in Russia are so used to cheating each other. The Communist system took care of that. The state cheated the citizen. No wonder men and women cheated on each other." Since Soviet governments repressed religion, churches couldn't offer an opposing view.

Many people really did follow the government's puritan dictates. In the mid-1970s, the sexologist Lev Sheglov traveled around the Soviet Union on a government speaking circuit. He lectured on sex under the guise of programs with titles like "Problems and Potential of the Contemporary Family" and "Harmony Among Spouses." I meet Sheglov at his comfortable apartment in St. Petersburg, where he's now the director of the respected Institute of Sexology and Psychology. "In the sixties it wouldn't have been possible, but by the mid-seventies the regime was calcifying. It had no more will left inside of it," he tells me. The auditoriums, factories, and local "palaces of culture" he spoke in were packed to capacity. "This was the only way to get information on sex. It was an exotic issue at the time," he recalls.

Sheglov was careful in his lectures not to compare Russia to the West or refer to sex outside the family unit. There were sometimes government informants in the crowd. Still, his lectures were rollicking evenings. A few old people usually stood up and shouted at him for being morally depraved. The rest of the time, usually half the audience giggled like schoolchildren while the others sat rapt, waiting to hear what he'd say next. Sheglov remembers a woman in a provincial city who said she turned her boyfriend in to the police after he asked her for fellatio. She wanted to know if Sheglov thought she had done the right thing.

"I tried to explain that you could ruin this man's life," he recalls, adding, "I understood that the society they had grown up in had made them this way. You can't just dismiss this woman as a fool."

WHEN THE Soviet Union collapsed in 1991, sex thundered out of the closet. Russia changed from a place where citizens could barely talk about sex to one where sex was a commodity. Suddenly Russians could watch all the pornography they wanted, rent hotel rooms with impunity, and find prostitutes in the newspaper. There wasn't any intelligent national discussion about sexuality, nor was there sex education in schools. But possibilities for sex were everywhere.

Lots of people had trouble adjusting. In 1992, when one of the first Russian soap operas came on the air, a lead actress refused to say the line "I want to go to bed with you." The scene had to be rewritten. On the same show, an actor was so enraged that his character was supposed to have an extramarital affair that he had himself written out of the script through a car accident. At the last minute, however, he considered his paycheck and decided to stay on the show.

The social rules changed quickly. Sexual relationships went from being a way to escape from real life to being one of the fastest ways for young women to become upwardly mobile. People who lived through this period tell me that in a matter of a few years, or maybe just a few months, it became acceptable for nineteen-year-olds to be seen on the arms of men several decades older. Perhaps not all Russians wanted their own daughters doing this, but it was hard to fight the new capitalist logic. The divorce rate soared as people got out of marriages they'd been stuck in since their early twenties.

With Russians suddenly free to emigrate, foreign men offered another route to prosperity. Love was optional. An American who taught English in Moscow tells me that during a class presentation a young woman recounted how her friend Maria married an American man, had a child with him, then turned around and divorced him. Maria is now in America, living off the alimony and child support she collects from her former husband. In the class discussion that followed, the storyteller's classmates praised Maria for her "cleverness" and castigated the American husband for allowing himself to be duped.

In this reborn society, whether you joined the new middle class or were left behind depended partly on luck. People who happened to live in central Moscow suddenly owned prime real estate. Others snatched the spoils of privatized companies and state industries. The men who grabbed the most, often through semilegal transactions, set the example for everyone else. These "oligarchs," who were resented but admired, ditched their Soviet-era wives and took up with younger women or entertained harems of gorgeous prostitutes. Their bacchanalian bathhouse parties quickly became the stuff of urban legend.

Not everyone could bed an oligarch, but below them were restaurant owners, advertising executives, building contractors, and employees of cellular-phone companies who offered a shortcut to the good life for fresh-faced young women. I meet several of these women, each with more perfectly chiseled features than the last. Many started as secretaries (the help-wanted ads for secretaries often specify that applicants must be attractive). The loveliest of all is Elena, a svelte twenty-eight-year-old with taut skin and feline blue eyes. In 1992, when she was sixteen, she left the provincial city where she'd grown up and moved in with an aunt who lived on the outskirts of St. Petersburg. She was soon a secretary at a computer-equipment firm, and it wasn't long before the owner, who was forty, was giving her rides in to work and offering to rent her the apartment he owned inside the city.

When he proposed that they move in together, the only glitch was his wife and sixteen-year-old son. His wife had been paralyzed from the waist down in an accident, so naturally, explains Elena, he was planning to leave her eventually. But Elena insisted that he speed up the process, since she wasn't the type of girl who would live with a married man. Also, Elena was pregnant.

"It was a very tragic situation," she tells me now, looking magnificently wistful. "I don't want to look like some bad person. . . . I obviously became quite upset. I felt for this woman. I have a sense of female solidarity." Her feminist impulses were no match for the economy of the new Russia. The owner ditched his disabled wife and married Elena.

Money is the great dividing line in the new Russia. As Emil Draitser observes in his book *Making War, Not Love,* adultery jokes in the 1990s show hapless husbands who are powerless to stop their wives from cheating with richer men.

> A man goes to a doctor: "Doctor, you know, every time I catch my wife with a lover, I drink a cup of espresso."
> "So what is your question for me?"
> "I'm worried that I'm getting too much caffeine."

In another the husband is similarly hapless:

"Can you imagine? I come home from work in the evening, and I catch my wife in bed with some Swede."

"And what do you tell him?"

"What can I tell him? After all, I don't know any Swedish."

Russians' obsession with sex and money, combined with the shortage of hard data about sex, perhaps inevitably led to the creation of the Institute of Soitology in St. Petersburg. Promotional materials claim that the institute does sex research based on "patrimonial knowledge of Slavonic coitis" (its name is derived from the Russian word for coitus). Over e-mail the director, a former philosopher named Neonilla Samukhina, assures me that affairs are one of her areas of expertise.

It takes me several weeks and many e-mails to set up an appointment, but when I arrive, the whole operation seems to be contained in one fluorescent-lit room. Samukhina, a heavyset woman with a lot of makeup, and the resident sexologist, a thin, dour-looking man in a black suit, are sitting behind a long table that's peppered with small fertility statues. On the wall over their heads is what seems to be an abstract pink oil painting but on closer look turns out to be a three-dimensional rendering of a vagina.

Our meeting goes on for about two hours, at the end of which I still have no idea what the institute does. Its general mission seems to be to make Russians take sex more seriously, with "no snickering," and "looking at sex as a cultural phenomenon." Samukhina describes the institute's various divisions, most of which she heads. The publishing division is particularly curious: She hands me an oversize hardcover they've published, with pictures of tanned naked couples having sex in various natural settings. (Chapter titles include "On the Ground," "In the Forest," and "On the Beach.") Captions describe the action in breathless terms.

The most promising part of the institute is its "advisory" arm. Samukhina wants to be a consultant to companies, on the topic of sexual harassment. This isn't to train managers not to harass their employees—it's to warn secretaries that they'll eventually be called on to offer "sexual services." Her advice is that if they're not willing to sleep with the boss, they should leave the company, because they have no legal protections.

Samukhina's expertise on affairs turns out to be rather perfunctory. Her main point is that cheating isn't just about sex but points to deeper problems in a relationship. "In Russian there's an expression: 'When things are good, you don't look for something better,'" she says.

ONE REASON there's so much adultery in Russia is that there are so few men. Since the 1980s the average life expectancy for Russian men has fallen from sixty-five to fifty-eight. They die of alcoholism, cigarettes, job injuries, and car accidents. By the time men and women reach sixty-five there are just 46 Russian men left for every 100 women (compared with 72 men for every 100 women of that age in the United States).

These skewed demographics infect romance. In Moscow I have lunch with a well-off single woman in her forties who tells

me that if she didn't go out with married men she'd have almost no one to date. In fact, she doesn't know any single
women who don't date married men. And none of them try to
hide this. For Russian women in their thirties and forties, let
alone older ones, a man who isn't married or an alcoholic is as
rare as a Fabergé egg.

Men flaunt their demographic advantage. A psychologist
named Alexei Zinger describes the etiquette: "On Saturday
night he may not come home. He says to his wife, 'Don't call
me, I'm going to be with friends. If you call, you'll disturb us.'"
In America this would be grounds for obsessively dialing a husband's cell phone or hiring a detective to track him. According
to Zinger, however, Russian women "need to accept this behavior, because he feeds her, her children, everybody. She needs a
strong man, but a strong man can leave for one or two nights."

The reality of this hits me when I go to interview a sociologist
at her apartment in Moscow but end up spending more time
talking to her charming eighteen-year-old daughter, Katya.
Katya is tall and skinny, with a pageboy haircut and a preco-
cious command of English. She's animated and confident, especially when describing what she wants in a husband: someone
who doesn't drink or beat her. She says she'll be lucky if she
finds someone like this. She's just a few years shy of marrying
age. Though she has the occasional fling, there are no significant
prospects on the horizon. Boys her age are "very cruel, and they
drink." The few serious ones are more focused on their careers
than on relationships, and there's a lot of competition for them.

Katya is so delightful that I want to reassure her that the right guy will turn up. But, considering the numbers, it's unlikely. If she does manage to find someone she can tolerate, fidelity would be almost too much to expect. "For me, of course I would like my husband to be faithful, and I will do the same, but I don't know, it depends on the situation. But if we have a good relationship as family partners, we have children, then if he has someone on the side, I have someone on the side, it's okay, so that the child will grow up in a family with both parents."

On the other end of this demographic divide are men like Sasha, fifty-four. In another context Sasha might be at a competitive disadvantage. He's just over five feet, with short legs pushing up a paunch. As an actor with a Moscow theater company, he usually plays the guy who pines for the beauty but loses out to the handsome lead.

In real life, however, Sasha claims to be a Lothario. I meet him in his cramped dressing room two hours before curtain time. It's opening night of a play about a crew shipwrecked on an island of naked women. When I ask him about affairs, his eyes immediately dart to the red leather couch in the corner. "Strangely enough, they all took place here," he says. I must look skeptical, because he gets up to demonstrate. "You see, you can remove these pillows and extend it. . . ."

Sasha's wife worked in the costume department, but that didn't hinder him. He tells me he once walked into a meeting and realized he had slept with all three women there. "And then a fourth one walks in!" he exclaims, making large theatrical gestures. "It's a wonderful feeling, fulfillment—everyone is a relative!" His marriage wasn't so wonderful. After his son was born, Sasha wanted to play a lot of tennis. "She would say, 'Where are you going with your racket? I have to be here with the baby!'" The couple divorced.

Sasha recently got married again. His new wife is a ballet dancer who's twenty years old, about the same age as his son. So far he's been faithful to her, but that might end. "I keep thinking about it, because it's male nature," he tells me. "We think as if this one will be different, but it's the same, really." He quotes Russia's iconic poet, Aleksandr Pushkin. My interpreter translates the last line roughly as, "All we want is that forbidden fruit, without which paradise is not a paradise for us." Sasha smiles mischievously and quotes a popular Russian saying, too, which essentially acknowledges that because of his extreme demographic edge, he never has to grow up. "A small dog is a puppy till old age," he says.

GENDER RATIOS and economics aren't enough to explain the prevalence of infidelity here. It also helps that, like the French, Russians don't get worked up about lying. While I'm in Moscow, the Russian edition of *Cosmopolitan,* Russia's best-selling magazine, is running a primer for women on how to hide their lovers from their husbands. The author advises readers to invent a fictional hobby (she suggests membership in the nonexistent "Society for Global Warming"); to switch to sexy lingerie only gradually, so their husband doesn't get suspicious; and to "try not to look too happy. If you never sang in the shower, don't start now." There's no mention of any ethical issues. The article says having a lover makes wives skinnier, happier, and more self-confident.

These days Russians have new opportunities to cheat. Couples live in such tight quarters that it's not unusual for them to vacation with groups of friends instead of with each other. These breaks are the perfect setting for so-called Roman affairs, the don't-ask, don't-tell holiday flings that start and end on Egyptian beaches and at Black Sea resorts. Roman affairs aren't scandalous or an indication of a troubled marriage back home. They're just a way to shed some stress.

But the crucial factor seems to be the shared belief that men can't control their libidos. I've heard people all over the world claim that men (and sometimes women) aren't naturally monogamous. But in America and Europe, they're expected to rein in the impulse to stray. In Russia, however, the polyamorous instinct gets to run wild. Women tell me that while they'd prefer their husbands to be faithful, they don't really expect fidelity. And the fact that so much cheating goes on seems to feed the belief that it can't be stopped.

I hear that outside Russia's big cities some husbands don't even bother hiding their affairs. My only chance to investigate this is when I meet Vladimir, who hails from a village in the interior. Vladimir looks like an aging Marlboro man, with broad shoulders, creased cheeks, and a drooping salt-and-pepper mustache. He and two of his sons spent the last weeks fixing up the country dacha of my interpreter, Anna. Their fingernails are still dirty when I meet them at the Moscow train station, where they're about to leave for home.

It's pure chance that I've gotten to interview Vladimir, and it strikes me how unlikely it is that two people from such different worlds would meet and discuss sex. The conversation begins awkwardly. Vladimir is bemused by my questions. I get the basic details: He's been married thirty-seven years and has five children. Then I go in for the punch.

"Do you have a girlfriend?"

"No."

Pause. "*Did* you have a girlfriend?"

Another pause. "Yes."

There's a long silence as Vladimir bites into a sausage (Anna had told me he'd want a bottle of liquor, but he just wanted dinner). She and I both wait for him to continue.

"It was in my village, ten years ago. Everyone knows over there. She's still there."

I'll summarize: The mistress was a divorcée who did accounting on the state farm where Vladimir was a manager. They met at a farm party. She was "very temperamental," a quality he admires. He claims they had sex at her house every day. After two and a half years, he ended it "quietly" by telling her to start looking for someone else. Oh, and his wife supposedly knew about the affair from the start.

Russians, like Americans, seem to believe that married people shouldn't keep secrets from each other. But whereas in America that presupposes a harmless emotional openness and intimacy, in Russia it often means exposing harsh truths. "I told her immediately that I have a woman, and she didn't say a thing. She didn't like it, but she didn't say a thing," he says. "Why hide it? Later she would have learned from someone else, which is no good. There would be bigger problems."

According to Vladimir, the accountant wasn't the first. "I had a mistress in Kazakhstan, I had a mistress in the Ukraine," he says, now a bit more relaxed. Actually, there were many women in Kazakhstan, where he worked in the 1980s. And, as it turns out, he doesn't have just five children. There are also the twin sons he fathered with a married woman there. His wife knows about them, but his other children, including the sons who are over getting dinner in the train station's cafeteria, don't have a clue.

His wife had a lover once, too. Vladimir says he took it in stride. "What is predicted by fate has to take place," he explains.

Vladimir has leaned in closer to me, and we're grinning at each other. To my surprise, I realize we're flirting. When he doesn't show his crooked teeth, he has a rugged charm. Affairs are his relaxation, he says. And there's another reason to do it: "When a woman asks, you have to go ahead. You can't say no." Apparently this is a quote from a famous Russian song. How would he sum up his marriage? "Thirty-seven years and no problems at all. Because a mistress is a mistress, and a wife is forever."

I'm struck that Vladimir wants his mistress to be "temperamental." When I mention this to a Russian man I know, he chuckles in recognition and says he also likes women with "salt." Agreeable women are too bland. Michele Berdy, an American who's lived in Moscow for nearly three decades and writes a column on language for the *Moscow Times,* tells me she divorced her Russian husband in part because she couldn't keep up with his demands for dramatic confrontations. "Emotional life with lots of peaks and lots of valleys is considered a good thing. . . . They enjoy feeling nuts," she says. "They want you to throw a fit and say, 'Leave my apartment!' They want you to have ultimatums. They want drama. And they want you to keep them in line."

No Russians tell me they cheat to create drama. They say they long for heart-stopping, tear-off-your-clothes romance. I hear about a man who left an entire lilac tree on the doorstep of the woman he was courting. Given the grim realities of life in Russia, this fairy-tale passion might be sustainable only in extramarital affairs. "In Russia they say, 'A good love affair makes a family more solid,'" says Nicolas, a paint salesman from Saransk who's in his late twenties. "It means new relationships dissolve all those problems within a family. After you spend time with another woman, you feel guilty in front of your wife, and you start to treat her better. Sometimes I miss her and I want to get back to my wife."

Unlike French people I spoke to, Russians didn't imagine that they were entitled to private realms where they could do what they liked as long as their husbands or wives didn't find out. A spouse discovering the infidelity, and the ensuing drama, was part of the script. Russia was the only place besides America where men told me they confessed their infidelities to their wives, because they couldn't hold it in anymore. This had the added benefit of moving the script along to the point of confrontation. But unlike confessors in America, those in Russia don't usually risk losing their marriage or spending years in dreadful "cry talks." In fact, by raising the drama, they might spice up their marriages. Any pledges to become monogamous are probably just for dramatic effect. After Nicolas confessed to his wife, he waited a bit and then started seeing his girlfriends again. "The biggest treason is treason by soul, not by body," he explains. Imagine a whole nation of people drumming up this kind of emotional turmoil. It's enough to make you reach for a drink.

THE ONLY PERSON in Russia who expresses even mild moral qualms about infidelity is Lev Sheglov, the sexologist in St. Petersburg. He says he advises his clients to practice infidelity in moderation, like any other vice. "People ask me what to do about this, I answer the following: Mankind invented alcohol and tobacco for his pleasure, but for some it has become a terrible problem. Extramarital affairs are nothing really horrible or terrible, but a person who's healthy shouldn't be addicted to this kind of relationship."

Sheglov says the ideal would be not to have affairs at all. "But, in life, reality shows this is very, very rare," he says. "Probably you should really strive toward this. But it's very unrealistic."

Or is it? If there's a 50 percent affair rate for men, then presumably the other half of men don't cheat. So where are these missing men? I can't find them. The whole time I'm in Moscow, I don't meet a single person who admits to being monogamous. Granted, I've sought out people to speak to about extramarital sex. But along the way I've met others, too, and none of them "confessed" to monogamy either.

Well, there was one. He's a twenty-four-year-old named Dolf who works for a university in Moscow. He's been married for a year, to a woman from his hometown. Five minutes into our dinner, he declares that he is faithful to her. "I don't cheat, because I love my wife too much, and I respect her. If I do, it would be difficult to wake up in the morning." It's an impressive little speech. Dolf has lived in America and considers himself a Republican. Unlike most of the other people I've interviewed, he knows how much Americans disapprove of infidelity. I get the feeling he's pandering to me.

This feeling gets stronger when the waitress clears away our main courses and Dolf is on his third drink. He describes the series of affairs he had with married women, before he was married himself. There was the Siberian woman who worked in a roadside kiosk; she asked him inside for a vodka one freezing night, and they had sex next to the space heater. Then there was the obese American who fell in love with him; he might see her again soon. He mentions that a blow job from a Russian prostitute costs about $7, and intercourse is about $18.

In between these remarks, Dolf pauses to proclaim his fidelity again. "But I may cheat in an hour," he says this time, trying to catch my gaze. There's a big commotion about which of us should pay for dinner; he says Russian men never allow a woman to pay, but somehow I end up giving the waitress my credit card. Dolf asks me where my hotel is and insists that it makes sense for us to share a taxi home. I agree, but only because I'm reluctant to travel through Moscow alone at night. In the backseat of the cab, he proclaims his fidelity to his wife one last time, keeling over toward me. When we pull up to my youth hostel, I lurch out of the car and bolt inside, alone.

AFTER TWO LONG weeks in Russia, I realize that I'm probably the only person in the country who's thinking about infidelity or who thinks it might be a social problem. There are so many worse things going on: a huge spike in deaths from violent crime and car accidents, a lurking AIDS explosion, a perilous population decline, and endemic alcoholism. Next to problems like these, adultery seems almost sweet. After all, it's about pleasure and even love. Most of the Russians I met were so stressed by their financial concerns and small apartments that affairs were a welcome respite. At most they viewed infidelity as a vice, like smoking. Far be it from me to deny them this small pleasure.

Of course adultery causes problems in individual marriages. Like people anywhere else, Russians are pained when their spouses cheat, and especially when their partners leave them for someone else. But because women expect their husbands to at least have little flings, the small rifts caused by these affairs are easier to heal. One woman in Moscow told me that a cheating husband does penance for having a girlfriend by taking his wife on a trip, preferably abroad. What Americans would take years to recover from can be reconciled in Russia during the course of a package vacation.

Russians are as romantic as Americans. But their storybook romances involve lots of problems along the way, and they don't have happy endings. Russians expect romantic happiness to be fleeting. The American ideal of a married couple living happily and faithfully through old age just doesn't hold up here, since most Russian men die before their "golden years."

I'm about to move on to a very different country, where men live longer than in Russia, by nearly two decades, but where many of those men have ruled romance out of their lives completely. Often couples don't even share a bed. The next stop on my round-the-world tour of infidelity is Japan, where I aim to see if there's any sex at all.

mystery of the single futon

I'M IN THE bedding department of the hulking Tokyu department store, or *depaato* in Japanese, which sits above the even more hulking Shibuya train station in central Tokyo. Imagine Bloomingdale's set atop Grand Central Station.

As I noodle around the stacks of pastel-colored futons, a chubby salesman approaches. He's wearing a black apron embroidered with the English words HOME SHOW. To my delight, he has studied in New Zealand and speaks a cheerful if halting English.

I point out something that's obvious to the bedding salesman, who by now has told me that his name is Toru: There are only one-person futons available. The store also keeps Western-style beds in stock, he tells me, but those, too, are only in single sizes (what we Americans call "twin" beds and use mostly for children).

But wouldn't doubles come in handy? Doesn't anybody snuggle to sleep in this country?

Toru furrows his brow and lowers his head, in that distinctively Japanese gesture that suggests, "I'm sorry, I'm about to deliver information that will displease you." Double beds are by special order only, he says, but, as far as he knows, no Japanese person has ever ordered one. The only buyers have been foreigners like me. "They are all working at the embassy or something," he ventures.

Japan is the land of the single bed. Maybe Japanese couples push their futons together. Maybe they crawl into each other's single beds the way my grandparents did. But what they don't do, obviously, is share a mattress.

Is this significant? I'm wary of fetishizing Japan's sexual habits, as foreigners often do. I had seen that when I studied Japanese for three years and spent a semester of college in Osaka. Back then I even had a Japanese boyfriend named Yuji, who wore a cowboy hat and loved it that my name rhymed with "camera." Unfortunately for the purposes of my current research, Yuji wasn't married at the time. And there don't seem to be any national sex statistics.

I set up a manic schedule of interviews in Japan, arranging to speak to lots of ordinary people and sit down with experts from the government and with leading sociologists and academics. I make appointments with divorce lawyers and psychologists, and hire research assistants to search for statistics and articles about affairs.

I intend to get to the bottom of the mystery of the single futon, even if I have to burst into Japanese bedrooms. Are couples here having regular sex with each other? Are they celibate? Or are they, as I suspect, off shagging other people?

I SET OUT with a novice interpreter named Maiko, who, despite the fact that she gets the giggles whenever anyone mentions sex, charges the egregious fee of twenty dollars an hour. Our first appointment is with a "marriage adviser," whose office is in a tony Tokyo neighborhood where trees droop over low wooden fences. I imagine the kids inside the sprawling houses here rushing to the door when their fathers arrive home holding briefcases and shouting *"Tadaima!"*—the greeting that means literally "I've come back!"

When we arrive for our appointment, Maiko and I put on slippers and enter a hygienically clean room to meet Hiromi Ikeuchi. Ikeuchi is a cheerful, petite woman in her mid-forties with a perfectly tousled bob and a fresh coat of red lipstick. Within minutes she tells us that she's divorced. This is, in fact, her calling card. "I like divorce! I love divorce!" she says. It turns out that her specialty is divorce, not marriage. The pamphlet she hands us explains that her office is called the Tokyo Family Lab—Research Section, which explains the quasi-surgical atmosphere.

On a white marker board, she draws a kinship chart showing the Japanese characters for "wife" and "husband" separated by a red line. The husband is the head of the Japanese household, called an *ie* (rhymes with "eBay"). When a woman marries, she's appendaged to her husband's *ie,* and her status shifts from "woman" to "wife." Ikeuchi draws more red arrows showing that the couple's children are born into their father's *ie* while their mother always remains on the other side of the red line.

No one writes love songs about the *ie.* It has more to do with property and responsibility than love. The *ie* is the opposite of the American marriage, where couples aspire to communicate and work on "the relationship." Ikeuchi says some older Japanese husbands don't even use their wives' names and instead address them with a crude form of "you." Even younger couples begin calling each other the Japanese equivalent of "Mother" and "Father" (or the marginally more modern *Mama* and *Papa*) after a child is born.

And then there are the single beds: "Mother" typically moves her futon into the baby's room and sleeps there until he's five or six (according to tradition, her husband replaces her in the master bedroom with a large stereo system and a flat-screen TV). Even younger couples who think the formal *ie* system is old-fashioned retain some of its trappings, snuggling be damned.

I tell Ikeuchi that none of this sounds very sexy to me. She agrees. That's why they call it "sexless marriage," she says.

Sexless marriage? Isn't that a contradiction in terms?

Not in Japan, she says. "Sexless marriage" (or the abbreviated *"sexress"*) describes Japanese couples who either have very little sex or no sex at all, particularly after their first child. It's a kind of syndrome that afflicts couples as young as their twenties and thirties and can last for years or even forever, usually without the couple ever mentioning the "problem." Hiromi isn't sure how many Japanese marriages are *sexress,* but she suspects the problem is endemic. She blames the *ie* heads, some of whom take a strange sort of pride in having a chaste marriage. "There are certain men who believe you don't bring sex and work into the home," she says.

That solves the first part of the mystery. There's not much sex at home. But is it happening someplace else? Or have I found a sexual culture without sex?

MY SEARCH FOR the missing sex in "sexless marriage" takes me to the conference room of a midsize Tokyo construction company. I have asked my contact at the firm if I can speak to some men there. Suddenly I find myself with an embarrassment of riches: five men in their thirties and forties, all willing to discuss their marriages, albeit all at the same time.

Like Ikeuchi, they'd rather talk about divorce than marriage. As they go around the room introducing themselves, I realize that they are all divorced, and in each case the men's wives ended the marriage. (Japanese women initiate most divorces.) When I ask what happened, the men throw out facile explanations—their wives fought with live-in in-laws or became more interested in the kids. I wonder what they're not telling me.

Finally one of the men, a forty-year-old quality-control specialist named Mamoru, confesses he was baffled when, after two years of what he thought was a happy marriage, his wife handed him a "green paper" for divorce.

"She said, 'Your name, please, sign, please,'" recalls Mamoru, who's dressed in the *salaryman* uniform of blue suit, white shirt, and striped blue tie. In the year that followed, he held on to the green paper without signing it but didn't ask his wife why she wanted to divorce him. In fact, they didn't speak at all that year, despite living together.

It's even harder for me to envision a talk-free breakup than a sexless marriage. But Mamoru says he feared that discussing the relationship with his wife would be more unpleasant than splitting up with her. "I was afraid to ask the reason. I was afraid that my personality might be destroyed," he says.

Whatever their inner struggles, *salarymen* like Mamoru aren't known for being sensitive or sexy. In the popular imagination, they have beer breath, premature paunches, and wear scratchy polyester suits. Employees of Goliath companies like Mitsubishi and Nomura get prestige from their jobs. But, at least according to the stereotype, most *salarymen* are corporate drones who haven't had time to develop interests outside work or learned to charm women.

The *salarymen* I meet in Tokyo do have one of the best opportunity structures for affairs that I've seen anywhere. They spend much of their free time carousing with each other. James Farrer, a sociologist at Tokyo's Sophia University, tells me, "If you go to a party in America and you don't bring your wife, you're asked, 'Why is your wife not here?' Your leaving her at home is a kind of insult to her and an insult to your marriage. Whereas here, to bring your wife to a lot of social occasions is seen as really out of place and inappropriate."

The intimacy and openness that's supposed to be the glue for American couples isn't something most Japanese couples strive for. Some men tell me they take pride in never sharing even crushing work problems with their wives. "I'm perfect to my wife. I give my love to her, but I never talk about my problems. I'm strong with her, I'm a perfect man," one Tokyo husband boasts.

Yoko Itamoto, a matchmaker who conducts state-funded field research on marriage, says husbands and wives often grow so distant that sex seems embarrassingly personal. "We start to have a sense of sex as a dirty act—the physicality of it, the liquid, people touching each other. Both men and women get this idea," Itamoto says.

AND YET these husbands and wives must crave intimacy with *someone.* But with whom? The five divorced men soon mention "hostess bars," where businessmen pay by the hour to talk to young women. Big cities like Tokyo are peppered with hostess bars, and there's usually at least one near the train station in any small town. Companies foot the bill at high-end clubs where their executives entertain clients.

"I prefer conversation with a hostess rather than with my wife," says the project manager, forty-two, who was married for a decade. "Between Japanese couples we don't have good conversations. They don't make jokes. But [hostess] girls, they know how to make jokes and have a good conversation."

Feeling like a charmer doesn't come cheap. On top of the hourly rate, a customer might also pay a "choosing fee" (if he wants the same hostess he had last time), a "karaoke fee," a "sitting fee," a "bottle fee," and a "snack fee." (One reason foreign men are kept out of these clubs is that they complain when these extra charges appear on their bills.) When conversation inevitably wanes, hostesses take out their cell phones and show the customers pictures of their pets. After customers leave, the women program in the men's birthdays and other personal details, to remember for the next time.

The hostesses seem to be a mix of call girl and therapist. Their aim is to make the men grow emotionally attached. Japan doesn't have much of a psychoanalytic culture, but at hostess bars men open up about their wives and families. A standard complaint is the lack of sex at home. That's also a nice segue into the main topic of conversation at hostess clubs: sex. As the night goes on and the "bottle fees" mount, the innuendos about sex turn to full-fledged conversations about it. One favorite trick is to teach the hostesses new expressions for sex acts.

But the missing sex from sexless marriages isn't here. There's almost no actual sex in hostess bars. A few have a "touch time" policy, which means that when the lights go out, customers can fondle the hostesses' breasts. But, in general, sex is bad for business. Profits depend on getting repeat customers, and the hostesses find that customers lose interest after they've slept with them, says Joan Sinclair, who photographed Japanese fantasy-sex clubs for her excellent book *Pink Box: Inside Japan's Sex Clubs.*

For reliable intercourse, customers, who tend to visit clubs in groups, have to move up the ladder to a sex club. They have plenty to choose from. In Tokyo's Kabuki-cho neighborhood, different kinds of sex clubs are stacked like brightly lit Legos in high-rise buildings and go on for as far as I can see (in between are the noodle shops, where, I figure, the customers go to regain their strength afterward). Nearby are Japan's famous "love hotels," where couples can rent rooms without coming face-to-face with a clerk. The hotels have different rates for a three-hour "rest" and an overnight "stay," and they advertise in-room services including video games, karaoke, and satellite porn channels.

Like the hostess bars, sex clubs offer varying levels of "service" that go far beyond the lap dances and champagne rooms of American topless bars. A variety known as "fashion health" specialize in massages that culminate in oral sex. "Soap land" clubs permit intercourse. There are extra charges for swallowing sperm, being allowed to ejaculate multiple times (standard charges cover just one ejaculation), and something called *soku-shaku*—in which the customer doesn't shower before he gets a blow job (this apparently heightens intimacy). If customers aren't sure what kind of club a place is, they can ask a tuxedoed bouncer whether it's *nuki ari,* a euphemism that translates literally as "to be uncorked" but in this context means "Can I ejaculate here?" (Foreign men are almost always told no.)

A special variety of *nuki ari* clubs cater to *salarymen* whose sexual imaginations are shaped by their commutes. Imagine getting off a crowded subway train and walking into a sex club only to discover . . . a mockup of a crowded subway car. In this subway, however, you're allowed to feel up the pretty women. Ten male customers and ten women enter the *chikan-densha,* or "pervert train," at the same time. (Women are supposed to shout "*Chikan!*" to embarrass the culprit if they're felt up on a real subway.) There are also mock parks, schoolrooms, and restaurants where customers can have a sure thing, making up for those dates they never had or the ones where they never made their move. When things get really heated in the faux movie theater, customers and their "dates" retreat to a private room, where a menu on the wall lists available "services." Sinclair discovered erotic tea ceremonies, a place called Club Mammoth that is filled with naked fat girls, and a club where the women pretend to be "somebody else's wife."

It's hard to know how many *sexress* husbands find consolation in Japan's sex industry. One economist estimates that Japan's sex industry brings in about $20 billion annually, a figure which doesn't include DVDs, magazines, and Internet pornography. The industry has grown so much that sex workers even have their own labor union. What's clear is that the whole discourse about sex is different in Japan. Most American men probably wouldn't tell coworkers that they have sex with prostitutes dressed in schoolgirl uniforms. In Japan, however, there's often no need to pretend that your marriage is the center of your sex life. Men who go to even the most bizarre sex clubs aren't considered perverts or sexual deviants. They're just boys out for some fun. The fact that they're probably all drunk at the time gives them additional cover. "It's a game," says Masahiro Yamada, a sociology professor at Tokyo Gakugei University.

The game gives husbands a break from being the "strong" man who leads the *ie* and shoulders the burdens of work. "The Japanese take dependency very seriously," a professor at Kyoto University tells me. "The adulterous relationship here is one without responsibility—that is its attraction."

JAPANESE MEN are continuing a storied tradition. In the seventeenth century, Japan's shoguns quarantined prostitutes into special neighborhoods, in part to tax them more effectively. The Meiji government, which in the late nineteenth century began opening Japan to the West, made these prostitution quarters into well-regulated business zones. For nearly half a century after that, visits to sex clubs essentially had the state's imprimatur.

It wasn't until 1947 that Japan's government outlawed certain aspects of prostitution, such as soliciting business or pimping. But the new law still allowed a man and woman inside a brothel to strike a private agreement for sex. This loophole continues to be widely used. Only vaginal intercourse even counts as prostitution; clubs with the right license can sell oral and anal sex, and anything else that doesn't involve intercourse. When a "delivery health" club dispatches a woman to a customer's house, technically speaking the two decide what to do only once she's inside.

Whether such encounters count as infidelity depends on who you ask. I don't hear about any Japanese marriages breaking up over a husband's encounters with "soap ladies." A divorce lawyer tells me that paid sex doesn't even meet the legal standard of adultery, or *furin*. Customers of these clubs apparently don't consider it *furin* either. Several people tell me there's a saying: "If you pay for it, it's not cheating."

Of course, it's better not to tell your wife you've just gotten a blow job from a half-clad "nurse" or that you've spent the evening talking to a hostess about her breasts. But men say their wives don't ask them where they've been. The wives apparently have a saying, too: "As long as he's safe, it's good that he's out."

A graduate student in Tokyo who is researching extramarital affairs tells me that wives believe "even the best husband, the most loyal, trustworthy, faithful husband, is promiscuous." That doesn't mean the women like it. She says housewives are heartbroken over their husbands' infidelities, but the practice is so entrenched that many don't think they're entitled to complain.

The don't-ask, don't-tell policy is wearing thin among some middle-class urbanites. One of the divorced men around the conference table at the construction company, a balding thirty-nine-year-old named Satoshi, tells me that after he got back from a business trip, his wife of ten years searched his bag and found a flyer for a call girl in Sendai, a coastal city two hours north of Tokyo. He says his wife got the wrong idea. The call girl wasn't anyone special, he'd had lots of women just like her! His wife didn't understand that it was just, well, play. "I don't have feelings for these women that I pay. It's a dry relationship—businesslike," he tells me.

More than being bothered by the infidelity, his wife seemed to envy her husband's freedom. After she found the flyer, she made a new group of friends at her sports club and took up scuba diving. Before long, Satoshi got the green paper, too. "When women think and have their own life and initiatives, it becomes difficult to get along all the time," he explains.

Satoshi has a new wife and says he's learned to prioritize his family over his job. He wouldn't go to a call girl now, would he?

"No!" he says emphatically. Then, with his coworkers looking on, he glances upward. "But I am going to Hokkaido tomorrow . . . to play."

WHAT ABOUT WOMEN? Are they having sex outside marriage, too? Midori, a gorgeous forty-year-old with alabaster skin and a Farrah Fawcett hairdo, seems like a candidate for divorce. She hasn't had sex with her husband since she was twenty-seven. They don't talk much. ("He's the type to drink and go to sleep," she says.) Since her husband is the eldest son, they live with his parents. He's a salesman and isn't particularly strong or resourceful. ("If my husband and I were left on an island without anything, I'm the one who would go out fishing.") Mostly, she's come to feel like his mother, a description I heard from several Japanese women.

And yet Midori says she's contented with her marriage. As we sit at a well-appointed café near a Tokyo train station, she explains why: She has a lover. "You can have different kinds of love at the same time. With my husband it's family love. With him it's the other kind of love," she says.

She doesn't expect romantic affection from her husband. "Mothers and sons don't have sex," she says.

Midori's husband assumes she's been celibate. In fact, once a month Midori and her boyfriend go to a love hotel. That's not even the best part of the affair. They *talk*. Her lover tells her about puppet making, his second career. This fascinates Midori. He's one of the few people she's known who was brave enough to give up a corporate career in order to follow his passion. On the deserted island, "he would be the one [to go fishing]. . . . He's the survivor, and my husband would be the spoiled rich kid."

Midori has manicured nails and a well-tailored black jacket that would be out of reach on a puppeteer's salary. When she got married at twenty-three, she was mostly thinking about finding someone who would one day care for her mother, who is divorced. Her husband said, "'You can rely on me.' I was asking for his assurance that he's not just marrying me but taking care of my mother as well."

The fact that her lover discusses his feelings has helped Midori understand what her husband's inner world must be like. "It's kind of strange, but because I started this affair, I started to respect my husband more," she says.

People have told me that Japanese people don't suffer from a Judeo-Christian sense of sin. (Fewer than 1 percent of Japanese are Christian; most practice a blend of Shintoism and Buddhism.) I don't really buy this until I ask Midori if she feels guilty about having sex outside her marriage. From her confused look, I see that she hasn't understood the question. When I repeat it, she's still confused. She's never associated infidelity with guilt.

The emotional stakes do change if a woman leaves her husband for someone else. One man I interviewed said his wife was so ashamed about leaving her previous husband for him that she punished herself by refusing ever to see her daughter again. My interviewee told me this in the course of telling me about his own affairs.

Midori, who has no intention of leaving, does have a very strong sense of propriety. She remains loyal to her husband by hiding the affair and not letting it interfere with her duties at home. Her husband hasn't been as discreet. Eight years ago Midori was in his car and found a man's purse that he'd received as a gift. He confessed that it was from his lover. Midori was furious, not because he had betrayed her but because he let her find out. "He broke the rules. Because if you have an affair, you're not supposed to let the other person know. No matter what happens, you shouldn't let the other person find out," she says.

Midori's arrangement starts to make more sense after I watch *Winter Sonata,* a Korean soap opera that's one of the most popular television shows in Japan, while I'm visiting. When the star of *Winter Sonata* arrived at Tokyo's Narita International Airport, the thirty-one-year-old with an unfortunate orange dye job was mobbed by throngs of his biggest fans: middle-aged Japanese women. Afterward, nine women were injured in the crush outside his hotel.

The show is about a woman in her late twenties who runs into the high-school sweetheart she had thought was dead. There are some twists: The former sweetheart (known in Japan as "Yon-sama") has lost his memory, he may be the woman's half brother, and she's engaged to his former best friend. But the main emotional storyline is that their love has been perfectly preserved during the decade that she thought he was dead, and even now it might never be consummated. To convey this, all the actors pose for their close-ups with an expression that looks like a constipated ache. It has as much subtlety as a bad love-song video.

Winter Sonata has struck a chord with the generation of women who, in Japan's lean postwar decades, married the workers who eventually powered an economic revival. They moved into the husband's *ie* and didn't ask questions when he arrived home exhausted at eleven at night and left again at seven. They may have had high-school sweethearts of their own, but they sacrificed passion for sturdy arranged, or at least "appropriate," marriages.

These weren't considered sexless marriages, because the

couples didn't expect to have much recreational sex. For the most part, the marriages weren't meant to be romantic. *Winter Sonata* touches a nerve because women of this age still dream of romance (and sex), but apparently not with their husbands (who, when they finally retire, are sometimes referred to as *sodai-gomi,* or "large chunk of garbage"). Their fantasy men— like Yon-sama—not only wouldn't spend their days barking drink orders from the couch, they might not ever be home at all. And that's okay. For these women the pleasure of a fantasy lover comes not from having him but from pining for him.

"You never know if they'll be together," explains Tamako, a fifty-eight-year-old divorcée who lives in Tokyo. Tamako is squat, with short hair and a contagious grin. She's a university graduate who, unusually for a woman her age, has a good job as an adviser to Japanese farmers.

Tamako thinks the Yon-sama craze is a little silly and insists she couldn't possibly lust after an actor who is the same age as her son. She adds that she's far too busy to take a theme tour of the Korean island where the program's teenage flashback scenes were filmed. (According to a Web site, "The cycling scenes from the movie are so popular that special *Winter Sonata* bicycle rentals are available to tourists who wish to ride along the same paths.")

But over Sunday-afternoon coffee in Tokyo, Tamako admits she recorded the previous night's episode and watched it this morning before meeting me. I watched it, too, at my hotel, and I can't resist complaining about Yon-sama's monoexpression and about the show's implausible story lines. (In another twist,

Yon-sama's mother has implanted him with a new set of memories that don't include his high-school girlfriend.)

Tamako isn't bothered by these details. "It's just that feeling I understand, it's not the story itself," she says. "Women in their seventies and eighties, they remember how they were young and in love." In fact, Tamako herself is enjoying a real-life version of *Winter Sonata,* except that the object of her longing is her own age and married. She describes him as "a regular *ojisan*"—or middle-aged man. They work in the same industry and first met twenty years ago, but they started their romance five years ago.

The man is not particularly handsome, and he'll probably be someone else's large chunk of garbage one day. What makes him special for Tamako is that he's virtually inaccessible. The two do a lot more pining than meeting. Because he lives an hour or so outside Tokyo and travels a lot, they meet only twice a year. In between they flirt over e-mails and text messages. (Tamako waits three days before responding to his messages, but, she says proudly, he responds to hers the same day.) She seems more excited about these exchanges than about their occasional trysts in hotels.

She doesn't mind that her boyfriend probably has a few other special someones. (He once thanked her for cookies she hadn't sent.) It still beats having a husband like the one she divorced ten years ago. "I like having this feeling of being infatuated," she says. "A lot of my female friends, especially college friends, are single. But they all have relationships, boyfriends. I don't know the details of their relationships. They just say, 'I have a man in my life.' I say the same thing."

The *Winter Sonata*–style infatuation with a love object who might never be possessed has deep roots in Japan's sexual culture. Anglo-Dutch writer Ian Buruma says "sadness" and "nostalgia" are the words that appear most frequently in both classical Japanese literature and in the country's modern pop songs. He also finds it in Japan's version of "chick lit." "Weeping tears of nostalgia is not something one comes across often in Western literature. Not that the emotion doesn't exist, but it is not usually so histrionically expressed; or, rather, what sounds histrionic in English is perfectly ordinary in Japanese."

Even more "perfect" than a love affair frozen in the past is one that ends tragically before it starts (*Winter Sonata* has elements of both). The extreme version of this is when lovers commit double suicide. These days in Japan, divorce is a lot more common. But the romance of double suicide lingers through the arts. Japanese stage plays from the Edo period (seventeenth through the mid-nineteenth centuries), which are still performed, were obsessed with double suicide. As Buruma writes, this was a time when "love so often ended in tragedy because there was no room in Japanese society for love. Marriage had nothing to do with romantic love."

It's hard to imagine a marriage in any culture living up to this extreme romantic standard. When characters from this period are asked to choose between their extramarital loves and their familial obligations, they opt to die with their lovers. The moment of their double suicide is the romantic apex of the stories. In *Sonezaki Shinju,* one of the Edo era's most famous Bunraku puppet plays, a courtesan suggests she and her lover bind themselves with her kimono sash before they commit suicide in a forest so that they will be "beautiful in death."

This fable still resonates for contemporary writers. One of the best-selling Japanese novels of 1997 was *A Lost Paradise,* about adulterous lovers who despair not only of ever being together but of the fact that even if they are together, their love will eventually become less pristine. To avoid this they commit double suicide while they're having sex (at the "peak" moment of their relationship, so to speak). As planned, policemen discover their bodies only after rigor mortis has set in. The couple literally cannot be pried apart.

TIMES ARE CHANGING in Japan. A few years back, there was a flurry of press about "Narita divorces." Women on their honeymoons discovered they were so bored with their new husbands that they dumped the men as soon as they got back to Tokyo's airport.

Today's brides are less content to pine. They'd prefer to meet and marry Right-san. And they want their marriages to be sexually exclusive. When I try out "If you pay for it, it's not cheating" on Ayako, a smart twenty-six-year-old who lives with her boyfriend, she replies in an e-mail, "Who said that to you? Must have been men who don't know women's feelings, in my opinion!"

Feelings are a big deal for Ayako's generation of women. When I ask twenty-somethings what they look for in a mate, their list almost always includes *tayori ni naru*—someone to depend on. A man who's *tayori ni naru* might work for Mitsubishi. He definitely has a nice income, and he leads the household. But he's a *salaryman* with a soul—a kind of emotional confidence and openness. Women still imagine that marriages consist of a quasi parent-child relationship, but in this newer conception they get to be the child. They envision their *tayori ni naru* mates as patiently listening to their problems and offering smart advice. "Someone who can support you, not just financially, but who can guide you when you're depressed, confused, or in trouble," Ayako explains. "This is really hard to find," she adds.

The problem is that while Japanese women are becoming more demanding, most men haven't evolved to meet these demands. Emi, thirty, an executive assistant at a French fashion house in Tokyo, is skeptical of men who claim they'd do household chores. "Before marriage, yes. But after marriage he expects the wife to support him," she says. "I've already heard some complaints from my friends about their husbands." Love marriages are the ideal, but when one Japanese magazine surveyed divorced people in their twenties and thirties about why they married, a third said it was *nantonaku*—for no particular reason.

Rather than settle, many Japanese women are choosing to postpone marriage. In 2000, 25 percent of Japanese women aged thirty to thirty-four had never married, compared to 7 percent in 1975, says Makoto Atoh, director-general of Japan's Na-

tional Institute of Population and Social Security Research
(who complains to me that his own thirty-year-old daughter
has just ditched her boyfriend). Women today are a lot more financially independent than were those who came of age in the
postwar decades. And they're influenced by the West: they
have degrees from English universities and own all six seasons
of *Sex and the City* on DVD. They don't want to live with the
husbands that are available in Japan.

Other women are trying to jump-start their marriages. Atsuko Okano is a Tokyo entrepreneur who runs a kind of charm
school for *salarymen* and their wives. She's the closest I've
come to an American-style adultery guru anywhere outside the
United States. The author of self-help books, including *Another Person Called "My Husband,"* Okano claims she's treated
about four thousand people over thirteen years of private practice. Half her clients are in sexless marriages and nearly all, she
says, are trying to win back a cheating spouse.

Okano, who's forty-nine and divorced, volunteers the fact
that she's juggling three boyfriends at the moment: a sweet-
hearted single guy in Kyoto who gives long massages on demand; a playboy type, twelve years her junior, whom she once
counseled through a divorce; and a fifty-three-year-old, about
whom she says woefully, "He's good-looking, he's strong, he's
intelligent, he has money. But, unfortunately, he has a wife."

Okano has figured out that both husbands and wives have
affairs because they crave intimacy, relaxed fun, mutual support, and sex. Her trick is to teach them how to get these things

from each other. At no point are the husband and wife supposed to discuss their relationship with each other or with a therapist. Okano brings in another type of expert: women from Japan's sex industry. Okano describes her call-girl consultants as if they're a team from McKinsey & Company. Who better to know how to please men and to teach them what their wives want?

When men come for training, the "soap ladies" teach them that their wives don't actually enjoy the kind of quickie encounters the men have in sex clubs. Soap ladies introduce them to mood lighting, candles, and compliments. "Women usually care about the ambience and foreplay. They don't want to have sex immediately. Men don't know about that," Okano explains.

Wives get an Eliza Doolittle–style makeover, beginning with a purging of oversize T-shirts and granny underwear. The soap ladies take them through visualization exercises in which the professionals describe what goes on inside sex clubs. They teach the wives how to cross their legs and behave coquettishly toward their husbands. It's a paradigm shift: Instead of shouting hello from the stove when her husband comes home, she learns to greet him with a full-body hug (perhaps spurring him to grope her butt, Okano says).

"The professionals teach them not sexual techniques but the process of reaching sex." Okano's three-month program (costing about $2,500) is for the usual cases, and the six-month program (about $4,200) is for cases where the wife "isn't pretty."

She supplements the weekly sessions with phone counseling. When a frantic wife calls to say her husband has gone to see his lover, Okano says she tells her to "stay calm. You'll get revenge later. Smile. Don't get angry with him; otherwise he'll dislike you even more." Throughout this process, husband and wife don't discuss the affair.

New lingerie isn't enough if the husband has a serious lover. In that case, Okano says, a wife must eliminate the competition. Okano's weapon of choice for this is shame. She coaches the wife to get her husband's boss on her side by making a discreet appointment with him to discuss a "business matter." She should bring an expensive gift. ("Japanese are weak when they receive gifts," she says.) When she tells the boss about her husband's mistress, she focuses not on the immorality of cheating but on how her husband is neglecting his obligations to his family. If the boss is sympathetic, or wants to keep the situation from getting messier, he'll pressure the husband to drop his girlfriend.

If this fails, Okano goes into shame overdrive. She sends an anonymous letter to the parents of the husband's lover, revealing that their daughter is sleeping with a married man. After the parents have had time to digest the letter, Okano stages an ambush. She, the wife, and some of her associates hide outside the parents' house, often waiting hours for them to come home. They approach the door, explain their purpose, and ask to come inside. There's usually a powwow in the parents' living room, during which the wife makes an impassioned plea for her marriage and children. The parents almost always agree to have a talk with their daughter about ending her relationship.

MY LAST STOP on the trail of sexless marriage is, in a sense, the beginning: a Japanese matchmaking party. It's the most awkward social event I've ever attended. Eighty people, about equal numbers of men and women, are shuffling around a large ballroom. The women are wearing mostly summer dresses, and the men are in ties and ill-fitting jackets. A banner spread above their heads reads SUMMER SPECIAL PARTY. They've paid about $63 each to be there, and most seem to regret it already. A cheery emcee has told them to mingle, but instead they've beelined for the beer.

It's almost impossible to imagine these people working up the nerve to have sex. They can hardly look at each other. The event's organizer guesses that one marriage could come out of the event but then scales back her estimate.

I approach a few people, partly to interview them and partly because they seem so desperate. Fumiko, thirty-eight, is thin, with black hair and splayed teeth. She works as a hospital secretary, though she'd like to quit her job when she gets married. I ask her what she's looking for in a man, hoping she'll say "a sense of humor" or "season tickets to the Yomiuri Giants baseball team." Instead she says, "Someone to depend on."

"Is it true that in America people just fall in love at first sight?" she asks me. Then she leans in and whispers, "Have you ever looked for someone on the Internet?"

I walk up to Sato, thirty-six, because he has a sweet face and because he's one of the few men not wearing a tie. He explains that he spends most of his time in his electronics shop, so he has few opportunities to meet women. His requirement for a wife seems easy enough: He wants someone who's "not nervous." In this crowd, however, that may be a tall order.

Hoping to help things along, I approach Junko, a thirty-three-year-old librarian in a flowered dress. She's standing alone on the fringes of the event, not far from us, and seems quite relaxed. If fact, she's just rejected a man who brought her a beer, because he seemed weak. "Japanese men are not aggressive enough," she says. She has trouble meeting potential mates, too. Just two men work at the library, and both are as old as her father. Despite the dozens of prospects now on hand, Junko scans the ballroom glumly. "Today I'm looking, but I don't see. They weren't bad, but I need something more." I'm tempted to tell her to cheer up. Just pick one and marry him. Your affair may be right around the corner.

I NEVER FOUND most of the missing sex from "sexless marriages." It's possible that the Japanese have less sex than any other people in this book. They don't have much of it in marriage, men seldom have it even in sex clubs, and even many Japanese affairs seem to be virtual, a matter of exquisite pining rather than actual sex.

I suspect that Japanese men miss sex. Certainly Japanese women do. The women aren't preoccupied with fidelity. But, like women all over the world, they long for romantic, sexually fulfilling marriages. Since Japanese men don't all share this vision, more and more women are choosing to stay single.

It's hard to blame these hapless *salarymen*. Once sex has been taken into the realm of pure fantasy and recreation, it's hard for real women—with their morning breath and emotional demands—to compete. Imagine spending the evening with your officemates eating sushi off the body of a naked young woman, then returning home to your wife, who may have some warmed-over chicken patties in the oven. The sushi wins out every time. But these days in Japan, the wife might decide she's reheated her last patty and get a divorce.

There's another, entirely different country where men routinely dally with other women as a form of relaxation and recreation, too. But in South Africa, cheating comes with a higher price tag than in even the fanciest Japanese sex club. Because of AIDS, the cost of cheating is often death.

we must have a
spare one at least

As far back as anyone can remember, medical workers in a South African township called Alexandra have been noticing a phenomenon that they dub "Alex syndrome." Poor black men, some as old as sixty-five, arrive at a clinic complaining of "impotence." But impotent turns out to mean that the men have enough strength to have sex only once or twice a night, every night. "They're frantic and beside themselves," a psychologist who worked at the clinic tells me. "Because they have a wife and a girlfriend. So they've been with the girlfriend, and they have to come back to the wife, and maybe they can only do it once."

The problem surely isn't limited to one township. Men in sub-Saharan Africa clock rates of extramarital sex that make even Russians look like prudes. In Mozambique, whose capital, Maputo, is three hundred miles from Johannesburg, 29 percent of cohabiting men in a 2003 survey said they had multiple partners in the last year, seven times more than married men in America or France.

Under what I'll call ordinary circumstances, one could debate the morality of routinely betraying a partner's trust, impregnating a woman besides your wife, and exchanging sex for money and favors. But things aren't ordinary in South Africa. One in five adults has HIV, the virus that causes AIDS. More than 1 million South Africans have died of AIDS illnesses. As I write this, the virus is a slow death sentence. Only a fraction of people with HIV have access to the antiretroviral drugs that could save them.

These facts have transformed cheating from a naughty hobby into a lethal practice. Infidelity acts as an extremely efficient superhighway that carries HIV through the population. When people have concurrent sexual relationships, the virus can jump to many different partners when it's at its most virulent. (People are most contagious when they're first infected.) In 1990, fewer than one in a hundred women who showed up in South African prenatal clinics tested positive for the virus. By 2000, one in four was positive.

"If you have high prevalence in a community, infidelity is a time bomb," says Allison Russell, director of the palliative-care team at Soweto's Chris Hani Baragwanath Hospital, South Africa's largest.

One common scenario is that a husband catches HIV from his lover, then comes home and infects his wife. Her children might then be infected as they pass through the birth canal or drink infected breast milk. If the parents are lucky, they'll live for another decade. But death often comes more quickly.

Given this macabre scenario, why do South Africans still risk cheating? Isn't the will to live and to protect their families a lot more primal and powerful than the desire to have sex with lots of different people?

IF YOU'VE NEVER traveled around the world trying to speak to people about adultery, you might not appreciate what a relief it was to receive the following e-mail from Isak "Sakkie" Niehaus, an anthropologist at the University of Pretoria. It arrived a few weeks before I flew to South Africa:

"Hi there Pamela, You have come to the right address. That is my specialty. Extra-marital affairs and AIDS. I have written loads about it. . . . Contact me as soon as you arrive."

Needless to say, when I arrive in Johannesburg, I make a beeline for Sakkie's office. Pretoria is about an hour by highway from Johannesburg. Under apartheid the university's student body was mainly white, but now it's 40 percent black and almost surreally integrated. On a blue-skied summer day, students cluster in multiracial groups along patches of grass in the main square, chatting and smiling as if posed for a catalog photograph.

Sakkie has a reddish beard and a deep voice that frequently erupts into a belly laugh. When I tell him that my round-trip taxi fare was about sixty dollars, he chuckles and says that's what a South African man typically pays the parents of his future bride. Considering my limited cooking skills, I wonder if I should I have forgone the interview and bought myself a wife?

Statistics on infidelity don't really capture the peripatetic rhythm of relationships in South Africa. But Sakkie has captured it in a "sexual biography" of his former research assistant, an amiable thirty-eight-year-old black man who lives in a rural district north of Pretoria, called Bushbuckridge. If the man, Ace, attempted similar behavior in Boston or Stockholm, he'd be considered a first-class cad—and he'd probably have some legal problems. But in South Africa his story is typical of someone who has a little bit of money and a lot of charm.

It's worth running through the highlights to show how changing people's sexual behavior would involve changing everything about their lives. Ace really gets going when he's nineteen and away at high school. He has relationships with five different women. When one of them gets pregnant, he denies paternity and flees to his hometown. Back home, Ace takes up with two more women: Helen and Iris. Iris gets pregnant. Ace gives her parents a thirty-seven-dollar down payment on the bride price. A brief period of faithfulness follows, probably the only time in his life that Ace will come close to being monogamous. But after a few months, he's hired to work at a mine out of town. His relationship quickly unravels. While Ace is away, Iris gets pregnant by the pastor of her church. She has an abortion. Ace finds out and beats her. Iris runs away from Ace and returns to her parents, taking their son with her.

The story continues like a Mexican soap opera. Newly single, Ace reunites with Helen, who by now is married to a

Nigerian doctor. Then he goes back to his job at the mine and sleeps with prostitutes until he meets a relatively well-off divorcée named Lindiwe, who is pregnant with her third child. Ace has lost his job at the mine, and he admits that he just pretends to love Lindiwe in order to get money and free beer from her. Eventually, associates of Lindiwe's ex-husband beat Ace severely. At this point, Ace is still just twenty-three (and thus middle-aged; the life expectancy for South African men is forty-three).

Ace then meets a woman who occasionally works as a prostitute, fathers three more children with her (he doubts the paternity of two of them), but beats her up and abandons her when (no big surprise here) he finds her with other men. Ace takes up with another woman who works in a clothing shop, but he soon discovers that she is also the mistress of a prosperous man with two wives. This turns Ace off.

Even for a man-about-town like Ace, all this running around is too much. He says he really just longs for Iris, the mother of his second child, since—aside from the small incident of being impregnated by the minister—she was always faithful to him. But when he finds Iris again, she is on her deathbed. After fleeing Ace she married a wealthy man who caught HIV from one of his girlfriends. He died, too.

IT's NOT IMPOSSIBLE to imagine people reining in their sexual behavior when they're confronted with a fatal illness. Gay men did. In July 1981, doctors in New York and Los An-

geles diagnosed forty-one gay men with a rare and deadly cancer. All the cases involved "homosexual men who have had
multiple and frequent sexual encounters with different partners, as many as 10 sexual encounters each night up to four
times a week." Of the nine men diagnosed in Los Angeles, several said they had been in New York recently. These men had
been living out the urban gay ideal. As John-Manuel Andriote
explains in *Victory Deferred: How AIDS Changed Gay Life
in America,* "Being gay in the seventies meant hot men, cool
drugs, pounding discos, and lots of sex."

Over the next three years, gay community groups formed
and used the gathering pool of medical information about the
disease to recommend how to avoid getting it. In 1984, the Gay
Men's Health Crisis, a grassroots advocacy group in New York
City, put out its first safe-sex guidelines. Gay organizations in
Western countries urged men to have fewer sex partners and to
use condoms and lubricants during anal sex. In New York City
in 1985, the health department began shutting down gay bath-
houses, which had been the site of much casual sex. Because
gay communities are concentrated in urban areas, many gay
men saw friends waste away from AIDS.

The sexual rules in Western gay communities changed.
Prominent gay men criticized promiscuous behavior. People
who flouted the new safe-sex rules risked being marginalized
from the only community that, for some, had ever fully ac-
cepted them. In effect, gay men policed themselves. "Behaviour change is less a process of individuals deciding to change

than one of communities changing their standards of behaviour and values," the Australian AIDS activist Adam Carr writes. He points to a 1990 Australian study showing that the more attached people felt to the "gay community," the more likely they were to have safe sex. Those on the margins or in the closet—and thus far from peer pressure—were at highest risk.

The result was that between 1984 and 1988, gay men in America reduced their number of casual partners by 30 percent, according to calculations by University of Chicago economist Emily Oster. That didn't stop HIV in its tracks, of course, but it slowed the spread among gay men.

Something similar happened among heterosexual Ugandans. According to a survey by the Global Programme on AIDS, between 1989 and 1995 the proportion of Ugandan men who said they had had at least one casual sex partner in the previous twelve months fell from 35 percent to 15 percent. Among women the proportion dropped from 16 percent to 6 percent. As with American gay men in the 1980s, "avoiding risky sex has become the community norm" in Uganda, the authors of a report explain.

Ugandans had the same information about AIDS that people had elsewhere in Africa. What seemed to change their behavior was how they got this information. Ugandans mostly learned about the disease from "personal channels"—friends, pastors, colleagues, and schoolmates. That is, like gay men in the West, Ugandans passed the safe-sex message to each other. "A credible communication of alarm and advice had taken root in discussions in social networks to a greater extent in Uganda," researchers Rand Stoneburner and Daniel Low-Beer write.

"Particularly in South Africa, there's just a really creepy silence about it. It's shameful or unacceptable or stirs up paranoid feelings," says Brent Wolff, an epidemiologist based in Entebbe, Uganda. "Whereas in Uganda they're not stigma-free by any means. But you're allowed to mention HIV without people thinking you're part of an international conspiracy or that you're making the country look bad."

In Uganda the health minister announced early on that the country faced a grave health crisis. In the late 1980s, Uganda's president backed a forthright campaign urging citizens to "love carefully" and practice "zero grazing"—codes for avoiding casual sex. (This didn't necessarily mean being monogamous, since Uganda allows polygamy.) Posters warned, AIDS IS GUARANTEED DEATH! BEWARE. Local churches picked up this message and spread it, too.

Uganda even had its own version of Rock Hudson, the American movie star who helped lift the taboo in America by announcing in 1985 that he had AIDS. Before Ugandan singer Philly Lutaaya died in 1989, he wrote songs about his battle with AIDS and toured the country speaking at schools and churches. His song "Alone and Frightened" still plays on Ugandan radio.

SOUTH AFRICANS don't suffer from a lack of information about HIV. Messages about safe sex are broadcast all the time on television and on the radio. There are free condom dispensers in university bathrooms. People I meet from all walks of life can parrot back the rules like passages from the Bible: Always use a condom or have sex exclusively with a partner who's faithful to you, too. In Johannesburg, public-service announcements implore people to drive carefully, since if they hit an HIV-positive pedestrian, their blood could mingle with that of the infected person at the accident scene.

Despite all these warnings, South Africans don't seem to have become more faithful. People continue cheating on their partners even though they know it might kill them. This goes against everything I thought I knew about human logic and the instinct for self-preservation. In 2000, researchers found that residents of one town were almost exactly as likely to be involved in an "ongoing casual partnership" both before and after a two-year HIV education program. Despite practically being experts on AIDS, just a third of men and a quarter of women in the township said they used condoms with their casual partners. (A paper about a township in the same area, published in an academic journal, is titled, "I Think Condoms Are Good, But Aai, I Hate Those Things.")

Economist Emily Oster looked at data from nine other African countries between 1997 and 2002, a period when information about HIV was spreading quickly. She found that the percentage of men who had extramarital sex fell only slightly, while the percentage of women increased a bit. Among all adults, men were just as likely to have more than one sex partner in the previous year, and women were only slightly less likely.

Although everyone knows what the rules are, it's also an

open secret that lots of people break them. Anthropologist Jonathan Stadler tells me that in the region where he did his field research, the joke about the Western "ABC" model for fighting AIDS ("Abstinence," "Be faithful," and "use Condoms") was that there should also be a D for "Death." He says no one was too scandalized when a youth AIDS awareness group's "Man of the Year" was found to have impregnated half a dozen women during his reign.

Although all of this made sense to South Africans, I still found it unfathomable. How can people trade a few minutes of pleasure for an agonizing death? I set off to explore this question up close on a family farm in Mpumalanga province, about two and a half hours east of Johannesburg. I get a lift in one of the owner's trucks. It takes a good twenty-five minutes of driving from the time he says we're officially on the farm to when we arrive at the office that's somewhere in the middle of it. All around us are fields of corn and potatoes. It feels like a long way from anywhere. About 120 families live on the farm, but their houses and a school for their kids are scattered so far apart that they have to catch rides from passing trucks like ours or walk long distances by the edge of the road. A few times a year, seasonal workers arrive to help with the harvests, and this is what probably brought AIDS here.

Though no one has kept death records, AIDS seems to have touched everyone. The first person I meet is Peter, forty-five, who's been a laborer on the farm for the last decade and lives with his wife and children. Peter is thin. A long scar divides his face, and a ratty argyle vest gives him the look of a dapper hobo. He tells me that his twenty-one-year-old son died two years ago and one of his own girlfriends died the year before that. In total he knows twenty-five people on the farm who have died of AIDS, most of them in the last five years. I'm told that some men treat their symptoms by consuming a remedy made of coffee, garlic, olive oil, chicory, and brake fluid.

And yet AIDS still hasn't achieved the status of fact. "A lot of people don't believe in it," he says. Death certificates list the cause of death as something morally neutral, like tuberculosis, though of course everyone knows this is usually a code for AIDS.

Peter insists he's changed his behavior as a result of what he's seen around him, but the changes are more in keeping with local lore than with the safe-sex rules broadcast on the radio. He hasn't, for instance, become faithful to his wife. But he doesn't have to, he says. Prostitutes on the farm now insist that men wear condoms. And "the girlfriends, you don't really pick up AIDS from them, because they're monogamous. Where a guy picks up AIDS is more from the whores," he says. When I point out that one of his girlfriends died of AIDS, he assures me that he won't be fooled again. "You judge her behavior when she's with other men. If you go and visit her and she's not home, you'd know soon enough."

Peter has a hard time following even these homespun rules. He says there are nights at the shebeen, an informal bar, when he has unprotected sex with prostitutes, too. "If we're pissed we don't worry about [condoms]," he says. "There are so many prostitutes, when a guy's not thinking straight, they pounce on him." The going rates are about seven dollars for one "round" and thirty-six dollars for a full night. There's also a monthly rate of seventy-two dollars (a real value!), which entitles the customer to nightly visits.

The line between "girlfriend" and "prostitute" is fuzzy, too. Peter says his last girlfriend left him for a guy who offered her more money. He says some female farmworkers are "freelancers" who become prostitutes at the end of the month, when everyone gets paid. For the rest of the month they may be someone's girlfriend.

As I look around the farm, it's hard to tell that apartheid is over. The owners are white, and the workers are black. Jabhi, a jaunty young man who tells me he's the farm's "health representative," says there's a funeral that day, though he doesn't know who died or why. As far as he knows, no one on the farm has ever admitted to having AIDS. I mention I've heard that a public clinic in a nearby town has begun offering antiretroviral drugs. Jabhi hadn't heard this; he wants to know more.

I'm curious about the freelance prostitutes, so Jabhi offers to drive me to meet some of them. It's the middle of the day, and the sun is beating down. After about fifteen minutes of driving straight through an empty cornfield, I peer nervously at Jabhi. Where is he taking me? Suddenly a flatbed hitched to a tractor appears in the middle of the fields. On it are about two dozen young women who've spent the morning harvesting. They look like a modern dance troupe, in an outrageous assortment of mismatched skirts, tights, gloves, and hats, to protect them from the sun and the cornstalks. Some have painted their faces with pink and yellow sunblock or tied colorful scarves on their heads. The effect is dazzling. They're gorgeous, and practically everyone is smiling. When I walk up to the truck, they all start shouting to me at once.

Jabhi and I pull six of the women off the truck. With him interpreting from Zulu, they start telling me about their love lives. They're in their early twenties. All but one have boyfriends, and none use condoms with them. "I trust my partner. He's committed to me, he keeps telling me the truth, he never lies to me," one of the women, who's twenty-five, tells me.

And what about other men? "If I have an affair outside my partner, I use a condom," she says.

What does she mean by "an affair"? I ask the women if they ever have sex for money. There's a collective pause, then a woman with a red scarf on her head speaks for the group: "During the month, no. End of the month, yes!" They all break out in giggles.

"But we use a condom!" another chirps.

"We are suffering!" another of the women, also twenty-five, tells me. "When we need money, you're supposed to use sex, then you get money." She says they earn about $115 a month from farm work, but they need closer to $215 for their expenses. They'll earn about $29 for a two-hour romp, consistent with the prices Peter had quoted. When I ask where they do it, they point at the cornfields. I get the sense that they don't use the money for spa treatments, but it isn't for food either. The girls work outside all day. They want to have a little fun, a bit more than a life of subsistence. One woman tells me her dream is to have a husband and children. Another exclaims, "I want to be educated!" They are energetic and curious, and they want to protect themselves. "Tell us about HIV!" they say, and then, "Tell us about overseas!"

But the men who can afford to be their end-of-the-month customers are also the ones most likely to be HIV-positive. (The very poorest men aren't at high risk, because no one wants to sleep with them.) In a study of South African men and women aged fifteen to twenty-four, women were four times more likely to have HIV than men the same age. Women who slept with men just a few years older were the most at risk. It's a painful conundrum for a poor woman: The guy with the car and the job is exactly the one to avoid. It's hard to imagine that logic working on women anywhere.

The other chink in their strategy lies in the line they repeat as Jabhi and I walk off, as if it's an article of faith: "I trust my boyfriend!"

I STILL CAN'T make the mental leap: People will continue having dangerous sex, even though it could kill them and their families. But perhaps I've underestimated how important romantic relationships are in a place where, even without AIDS and apartheid, life is pretty bleak. Love, whether in marriage or an extramarital relationship, offers one of the few havens from the unemployment and violence that haunt most people here.

Compared with South Africans, Western gay men had it easy: They decided to forgo one-night stands or start using condoms with people they barely knew. In one-time encounters with prostitutes, South Africans have become more likely to use condoms, too. But in South Africa the most dangerous behavior takes place within relationships where people have feelings for each other, even if they're not monogamous. That makes it harder to insist on a condom.

"You could say the dynamics of human relationships are antithetical to condom use," says Brent Wolff, the epidemiologist in Uganda. Asking someone to wear a condom implies that you don't trust him, and you need trust to feel love and passion. Wolff says it's almost impossible to find anyone who uses condoms consistently in any country, even among people who swear that they do.

This conflict seems to haunt Khayelitsha, a metropolis of tin-walled shacks just off the highway between Cape Town and the airport. The township's population surged after the main apartheid laws were repealed in June 1991 and blacks were suddenly allowed to travel freely. Thousands from the poor Eastern Cape flooded into the area around Cape Town looking for jobs. Many never found them, as evidenced by the fact that plenty of Khayelitsha's roughly 750,000 residents still rely on outhouses and candlelight.

One of the most modern-looking buildings in Khayelitsha is a maternity unit. On the morning I visit, a room inside the unit is slowly filling up with women and their babies. The women are chatting with each other in a "clicking" language called Xhosa, which sounds like the movements of a grandfather clock. No one is breastfeeding. They're all in a mentoring program called mothers2mothers, whose founder, Mitchell Besser, an American gynecologist, wanted to teach HIV-positive pregnant women how to keep themselves and their children healthy. He tells me on the phone, "I think we've conceded fidelity, and we're just going for safe infidelity."

Coordinator Pat Qolo says on average one in four pregnant women who come to the clinic is positive. But of course not all days are average. Earlier in the week, half of the thirty women who tested were positive. On any given day, "it's never less than ten," she says.

One of these women is Zukiswa, thirty-two, who's sitting in a corner holding her three-month-old baby. Zukiswa is plump, with girlish features and a steady, intelligent gaze. She met her husband when she was a sixteen-year-old schoolgirl on the Eastern Cape and he was a thirty-six-year-old taxi driver who offered her driving lessons.

She says she's never "gone all around" when her husband was away, so she has a good idea where she caught the virus. "You know your husband sometimes doesn't sleep at home," she says. He knows she's positive, but he refuses to get tested. And though he promises not to go to shebeens, he still does. Some are no more than dirt-floored shacks, where beer is brewed in a large tub and prostitutes hover. Sakkie describes the shebeens as places of alternate reality where the ordinary rules of behavior don't apply. Zukiswa's husband expresses it similarly. "He says, 'You know when you are drunk, your mind is not in what you are doing, so you can do anything.'"

The couple's new baby will be screened for HIV next week. If the baby is positive, that may be all the more reason for her husband not to get tested. If his own status remains ambiguous, he can't really be blamed for infecting his wife and child. Even outside the shebeen, he can stay in an alternate reality, where the virus could have arrived in his house mysteriously.

Although her husband has disappointed her, in the eyes of his buddies he's done nothing wrong. If he stopped going to the shebeen, they'd think he was henpecked. Zukiswa seems extremely strong-willed, but she doesn't have the authority to break the hold that this kind of thinking has on him. "Our husbands don't want to be told by women what to do and what not to do. That is the reason," she says.

Pumza, who's sitting a few chairs down from Zukiswa, is less eager to blame her boyfriend for giving her HIV. She still swoons as she describes the day she met him on a street in Khayelitsha. "He was just walking, and he saw me, and he asked me, 'Where can I take you?'" she remembers, suddenly grinning like a schoolgirl. "Oh, he was a nice guy. He was beautiful and talking slowly."

Pumza, twenty-six, has short hair, luminous chocolate-colored skin, and intense brown eyes. I can imagine a man being eager to get her number. But two years after her future boyfriend chased her down the street, he was dead of AIDS. In the end he was so thin Pumza couldn't tell if there was anyone in his bed.

At first Pumza says she's not sure how she got HIV. She had another boyfriend before this one. Maybe it came from him? Then she mentions that after a support group the previous week, a woman approached her, saying she had dated Pumza's late boyfriend before Pumza met him. This woman found out she was positive in 1995 and told the boyfriend about it then. She had seen Pumza around Khayelitsha and had wanted to warn her. She told Pumza after the support group, "I didn't know even if you'd already been sleeping with that guy without a condom. But I was wondering about you. That guy, I know he is infected. I wonder if he told you that he is positive."

Pumza can't really reconcile this new information with that romantic day on the street when a handsome young man asked for her number. "All that time he was positive, all the time he was positive. The time he came to me, he was knowing he is positive," she says, almost to herself. But Pumza doesn't know how to blame him, especially since she is still grieving him. As suddenly as the new information came in, it seems to leave her. "I did blame him," she says suddenly. "But now I can't do otherwise, because he died."

WHEN I TALK to South African men about infidelity, they almost always mention the king of Swaziland. Swaziland is a tiny country landlocked by South Africa and Mozambique. Its leader, King Mswati III, is the last absolute monarch in Africa, and other southern Africans view him as an über-male. The king, thirty-eight, has legendary sexual appetites. Every year he chooses a new bride from among tens of thousands of young women who parade topless at a giant festival. While I'm in South Africa, local newspapers reveal that Mswati has spent $820,000 buying ten new BMWs for his current wives.

In addition to being extremely poor, Swaziland has the world's highest rate of HIV infections. According to *The World Factbook,* 39 percent of Swazi adults are infected (compared to roughly 22 percent of South African adults). The life expectancy for Swazi men is thirty-two; for women it's thirty-three. One can only imagine the various routes the virus takes. In 2000 the king banned Swazi schoolgirls from wearing miniskirts, to discourage sexual relationships between students and teachers. The following year he banned girls under eighteen from having sex at all but soon defied the ban himself by selecting a seventeen-year-old as his ninth wife (he fined himself one cow).

King Mswati claims—and many southern Africans seem to believe—that by having multiple wives he is upholding the region's disappearing traditional values. Ordinary South African men and women tell me their ancestors were polygamous, too, and that in the "old days" men didn't play around because they had enough women at home to satisfy their urges. These days, however, men have lovers because they can't afford to have more than one wife.

This account seems to be based on a misunderstanding of history. A pair of historians at the University of Witwatersrand in Johannesburg say polygamy was never widespread. Peter Delius and Clive Glaser write that only a small minority of pre-colonial southern Africans—mostly chiefs and wealthy men—had multiple wives. And polygamy didn't do much to contain their extramarital urges. "Extra-marital sexual liaisons were as 'traditional' as polygamy itself," they write.

Delius and Glaser explain that extramarital sex became more common in the 1930s as black couples separated so the men could work in distant mines. When their husbands were away, wives turned to a kind of sexual bartering that included romance and companionship as well as money. A 1930s observer of Johannesburg slums noted that "only a few women admitted that they had *nyatsi* (backdoor husbands), but all informants readily and emphatically testified that their neighbors had 'sweethearts.'"

This practice is still so common that men who pay girls rent in exchange for sex are dubbed "minister of housing," those who pay school and university fees are referred to as "minister of education," and of course the "minister of communication" loads airtime on their cell phones. (Men who buy food are known simply as "lunch boys.") Helen Epstein, a leading writer on AIDS in sub-Saharan Africa, points out that these gifts aren't strictly payment for sex. They're also a tangible proof of love.

One of those in a position to pay is William, forty-seven, who operates a furnace at a company in Cape Town called SA Metal Group, which has an innovative in-house program to treat employees with AIDS. William's sinewy body, high cheekbones, and jutting front teeth give him the look of a wizened beaver. He has been plucked from the furnace and plopped in front of me inside an air-conditioned office because he's one of his company's HIV "peer educators." This means he's supposed to set an example for his coworkers. But while William says all the right things about condoms, he doesn't even pay lip service to fidelity. "In our culture, if you like, you're supposed to have a girlfriend outside. Sometimes children as well. It's not a problem for our culture," he says.

It is, however, a problem for his wife. "I didn't tell her. I'm scared to tell her," he admits. Instead, about twice a week, he phones around 8:00 P.M. and says he'll be staying with his "brother" that night. His wife has never called him on the ruse. Though he has to operate stealthily, William is confident that what he's doing is correct. After all, there are nights when his wife doesn't want to have sex. And, like many men, he won't have relations with his wife while she is pregnant or nursing. "We men, we must have a spare one at least," he says.

That same message comes from on high. In 2006, Johannesburg's High Court acquitted former deputy president Jacob Zuma of raping a thirty-one-year-old woman in the master bedroom of his house in Johannesburg. Although the judge ruled that the sex had been consensual, he chastised Zuma for having had unprotected sex with the woman even though she was an AIDS activist who he knew to be HIV-positive. Zuma, sixty-three, is the former head of the National AIDS Council.

In testimony that kept the country rapt, Zuma, who is married, explained how this came to pass: "I touched her and kissed her. When I touched her private parts, she was ready." They discussed using a condom, but neither had one. Zuma said he hesitated, but the woman insisted that he couldn't "leave a woman in that situation," South Africa's *Mail &*

Guardian newspaper reported. "And I said to myself, 'I know as we grew up in the Zulu culture you don't leave a woman in that situation because if you do then she will even have you arrested and say that you are a rapist.'"

The woman then "opened her thighs wide, they kissed each other and then started having sexual intercourse." Zuma testified that he took a shower afterward in hopes of lessening his chances of contracting the virus. In court his lawyer defended this technique.

IN THE SOWETAN NEWSPAPER, the personal ads are right above the death notices. It looks like a deliberate metaphor for the fact that love has grown so close to death. The people on either side of the fold even seem to speak to each other. "Douglas M." writes that he is "a single man aged 25 with no children and am looking for a woman aged 18 to 23 without children who is ready to settle down. She should be well-mannered and respectful. . . . Please reply in English, isiZulu or Shona and enclose a photo." A woman named Lydia fits his description: She's twenty-one, apparently childless, and in her photo she's quite pretty. If only Lydia weren't going to be "buried on Saturday at the Avalon Cemetery." Next to hers are death notices for seventeen other people who should have been on the other side of the page: Most are in their thirties or younger. A baby-faced boy named Modiko is just nineteen. None give the cause of death.

How can anyone accept this? Emily Oster, the economist, decided to challenge the idea that people everywhere are equally eager to preserve their own lives. She postulated that middle-class gay men in America put a higher value on their lives than do poor Africans with less money and years to lose if they get infected with HIV. For both groups, she studied the period before antiretroviral drugs were available.

To measure this, Oster created a model for what she calls the "calibrated price of a sexual partner." This represents the years of life and income that someone stands to lose by having sex with more than one person during a twelve-month stretch. She calculates that when the HIV rate increases by one percentage point in certain African countries, the "price" of a new sex partner is $1,569 for women and $853 for men. For the mostly middle-class gay men in her sample, the "price" of having an additional sex partner is about $5,500.

Oster used data from Benin, Burkina Faso, Ethiopia, Ghana, Kenya, Malawi, Mali, Namibia, and Zimbabwe. South Africa, which is wealthier than most other sub-Saharan countries, wasn't included in her country surveys.

Consistent with her hypothesis, Oster found that richer people with long life expectancies changed their behavior more than did poor people with shorter expected lives, whether they were Africans or gay men in America. These results suggest that a man at a shebeen in a South African township weighs the risk of seducing the lovely woman in front of him against his joblessness and the fact that men around him die in their early forties. Give that same man a better-paying job and more years to live, and he's less likely to invite her for a tryst out back.

There is pessimism in South Africa. The marriage rate has plunged. Jonathan Stadler, the anthropologist, says men in the rural region he studies used to spend years saving up to get married. Now some use their layoff packages to buy out a bar for two weeks. I had expected stories about AIDS to run on the front pages of local newspapers every day; imagine if 20 percent of American adults had a deadly illness and they weren't getting treatment! But most of the articles about AIDS that I see run on the inside pages.

None of the people I meet suggest they are indifferent to their own fate, however. Many, like Lucy, a thirty-two-year-old cleaner in Johannesburg, are petrified of dying and desperately want to live long enough to raise their children. But the ubiquity of death has a numbing effect, too. Lucy's husband, father, and niece are dead from AIDS. When she learned she was positive, too, she merely said, "Yes, I know, I was waiting for that." Her husband had made her sleep on the living room floor while she was nine months pregnant, so that he could make love to another woman in their bedroom. When Lucy warned one of his lovers that he was HIV-positive, the woman brushed it off and said Lucy was jealous.

Lucy also blames herself for getting HIV. She says her husband probably wouldn't have become a "running man" if she'd been willing to do "that thing," meaning fellatio. Anyway, Lucy understands his need for a variety of partners. She had a relationship on the side with an old boyfriend who was married himself. "If you keep on eating the chicken meat always, it's going to be bad. You have to change the diet," she says.

The period when her husband got sick was also one of the best in their marriage. He finally calmed down, and they enjoyed each other's company. For a brief few months, there were no other women, and "I was sitting as a woman in my home," Lucy says. That peace shattered when he died and his family accused her of killing him with a love potion. "My mother-in-law said, 'Why are you not sick? You are supposed to get sick together.'"

There are so many different sets of rules circling Lucy that in the end she reaches for the most soothing one: A wife should love her husband, and people in love don't kill each other. When she thinks about her husband now, all she feels is longing. She remembers that on Thursdays he'd buy a chicken and a liter of Coke and have it at the kitchen table. "Now, can you believe it, I miss all the stuff. I miss even his steps when he came from the shebeen, when he walked like an old man. I miss all those steps now." She forgives him for cheating on her. She forgives him for giving her HIV. She forgives him for dying and leaving her alone. "I must forgive him, whatever he did to me, because God is asking him the questions now."

When Americans find out that their spouses have lied to them and were unfaithful, they're thrown into cognitive dissonance. How could a person who loves me have lied to me? They lose their bearings and decide that nothing in their lives is what it seemed. The experience is disorienting and painful. But at least it's not usually deadly.

South Africans long to trust the people they love, too. Even in a country where infidelity is rampant, wives hope that their little corner will be safe from cheating and disease. When it's not—when their husbands cheat and bring HIV home—their reactions often aren't rational but romantic. Women aren't thrown into cognitive dissonance, unsure of whether they've always been "living a lie." They cling to the starry-eyed view of their relationships. Who wants to give up love? Especially if you've just found out you're going to die.

I arrived in South Africa thinking that what matters most to people is survival. But diseases exist in the realm of doctors and science. The fear of dying often isn't enough to stop people from cheating. Rather, what women like Lucy and men like Ace seem to want is love, sex, and acceptance by their peers.

What about the fear of God? Does that keep people from cheating? Or are religious people also more swayed by their friends than by their God? To answer this question, I add extra pages to my passport (I've run out of room for new visas and stamps) and go forth to meet the faithful in several countries.

god in the bedroom

WHEN SHLOMO MET his future wife, members of both families were waiting outside the door. They had already researched each other's backgrounds, and it was up to the prospective bride and bridegroom to sign off on whether they would spend their lives together.

"We were in a room. We just said, 'How many brothers? How many sisters?' After five minutes her father came in and said, '*Nu?*' . . . My father, I asked him for another five minutes. Then I told him, 'It's fine.'"

Shlomo was eighteen and a half, and it was the first time he'd ever been alone with a girl other than a family member. "I learned in yeshiva, you cannot even think about girls. It's a sin."

After the wedding party some months later, both sets of parents accompanied the young couple home. The bride's mother took her daughter into the kitchen and told her about the birds and bees, while Shlomo got a similar talk in the living room from a friend of the family. Shlomo says the man told him, "I don't know what you know, what you don't know. . . . A man has a penis between his legs. She has this." He gave Shlomo several sheets of paper with instructions about precisely how to proceed. He and his new wife, who appeared to be in shock from what she had just learned in the kitchen, sat down together to study the rules. They included:

1. The couple should undress completely.
2. When Shlomo first thrusts inside her, he'll break her hymen and make her bleed. This will make her impure. So if he withdraws, he cannot reenter.
3. Since the bride will be impure, after Shlomo withdraws, the couple mustn't touch again for five to seven days.

It took several hours for the newlyweds to review all the instructions. By the time they got into bed, the sun was up. The bride was so scared she was sweating. Shlomo thrust inside her for a few seconds, but he was so self-conscious he withdrew, perhaps before going in far enough. Neither was sure whether they had done it right, so later that day Shlomo went to a "big rabbi." The rabbi listened to Shlomo's story and then pushed two fingers of one hand through a circle in the other hand, trying to establish how far Shlomo had gone inside his wife and whether his penis was "hard like a finger" at the time. Shlomo assured him it was.

"He decided it was enough," Shlomo recalls, still visibly relieved. "Even if you didn't go all the way, you did it."

Ultra-Orthodox Jews aren't the only religious people who get worked up about sex. By one count, 80 percent of Islamic law deals with marriage and women's behavior. By some accounts, the seventh-century rupture that split Muslims into Sunnis and Shiites was sparked by a dispute over whether the prophet Mohammed's youngest wife, A'isha, cheated on him or merely shared a camel ride with an attractive younger man.

Islam, Judaism, and Christianity all ban adultery in the most severe terms. The Ten Commandments forbid it and then implore followers not to covet their neighbors' wives. Jesus didn't want his followers even to think about extramarital sex. He said anyone who looks at a woman "lustfully" has "already committed adultery with her in his heart."

But none of the major religions take adherence to the ban on adultery for granted. A Catholic catechism acknowledges that "self-mastery is a *long and exacting work*. One can never consider it acquired once and for all. It presupposes renewed effort at all stages of life." The apostle St. Paul calls adultery the rebellion of flesh against spirit. Both Muslims and Jews resort to covering up women and separating the sexes in order to remove temptation.

But does all this attention to extramarital sex keep religious people from straying? Do the rules and roadblocks succeed in channeling people's sexual urges safely into marriage? Is the fear of God's wrath enough to make the faithful faithful—or at least more faithful than nonbelievers?

Statistics can't fully answer these questions. I decide to head out into different religious communities and look at people who are struggling with the tension between what religious laws say and how the people around them really behave. It's by no means a definitive look at any religion, but it shows the pressures and difficulties that are involved.

MY FIRST STOP is Brooklyn, New York. Brooklyn is a kind of Holy Land for the ultra-Orthodox Jews known as Hasidim, whose sects are clustered in neighborhoods throughout the borough. A trained observer can distinguish between adherents of the different sects by the types of hats they wear and the length of their earlocks, known as *payos*. Most Hasidim speak the dialect of Yiddish native to the village in Poland or Hungary from which their forebears emigrated generations ago. Unlike Jews who are merely ultra-Orthodox, members of a Hasidic sect take direction from their "rebbe," who's often part of a rabbinic dynasty that stretches back a century or two.

Satmar is one of the most exotic Hasidic sects. Though thousands of Satmar adherents live a short subway ride from Times Square, they might as well be on another planet. Some Satmar men wear the white kneesocks and round fur hats that used to be au courant among Hungarian aristocrats. Married women take the injunction to be modest so seriously that they shave their heads and then cover their bald pates with both a wig and a scarf. Many Satmar have only a rudimentary command of spoken and written English and just a sixth-grade knowledge of science, mathematics, and history. Few go to college: Hasidic mothers want their sons to be religious scholars, not doctors. By age twenty-one, women are considered so old they're virtually unmarriageable.

Once they're married, Hasidic couples (as well as some other ultra-Orthodox Jews) don't touch, hand each other objects, or use terms of endearment while the wife is menstruating, and then for another protective week after that. Doing so could incite the couple's lust and lead them to have sex while the wife is considered impure. Some couples are extra-careful and *never* say anything intimate to each other, even refraining from ever using each other's first name. One young man tells me his father called his mother *"Herr nor,"* Yiddish for "Listen up." I'm reminded of Japanese couples who just say, "Hey, you."

I've heard rumors that the Hasidic world isn't as chaste as it appears—or as chaste as Shlomo's wedding night would suggest. I'm told that some Hasidic men frequent prostitutes, and that they've even worked out religious loopholes to make this kosher. Is this just an outsider's fantasy? How will I get inside this closed world to find out?

Through a series of contacts, I finally make my way to a kind of Hasidic clubhouse where men from various sects, but mostly Satmar, hang out. It's on the second floor of a storefront building on the outskirts of Borough Park, which is home to one of the world's largest Orthodox populations. The clubhouse is a refuge for misfits of the Hasidic world—men who are so drenched in Hasidic culture they can't really leave it, but who need a place where it's safe to criticize it. Many have long *payos* and follow the injunction to not even flip a light switch on a Saturday, the Jewish Sabbath. But maybe they doubt the existence of God or they're hooked on watching the television series *24*. Others, like Shlomo, simply need a break from their wives' relentless piety. The clubhouse could use a good scrubbing (my parting gift to the organizer is a functioning lamp), but the atmosphere is lively and congenial. Kosher pretzels and pizza get passed around a lot, and clever men in black coats sit there telling jokes whose punch lines have to be delivered in Yiddish.

These men don't represent all religious Jews or even all Hasidim. But since most of them grew up in the peculiar cultures of the Hasidic world, they are intimately versed in what's acceptable and what isn't. One young man says he used to sneak into the public library to read novels; he got divorced even though his father warned him he'd be putting a stain on the family's reputation and that the stress was exacerbating his mother's cancer. (A divorced man can remarry but will probably have to settle for someone of "lesser quality," like a divorcée who has a child.) Another man at the clubhouse, an intensely handsome twenty-two-year-old with shiny black *payos,* says his real joy is dancing; he has memorized the choreography on several Britney Spears videos. But his father is pressuring him to get married, and he's running out of excuses. He fears that if he strays too far from the fold—if he starts even dressing differently, for instance—his parents and most of his thirteen siblings would stop speaking to him.

Although the Hasidim I meet have been cut off from much

of modern civilization, they are learned about sex. They've spent most of their adolescence in yeshivas, single-sex religious academies where they study the Talmud, sometimes for as long as as twelve hours a day.

The Talmud's more than twelve thousand pages of arguments, stories, and teachings on Jewish law contain rich discussions of sex. An entire book is devoted to the *sotah*, a woman whose husband suspects her of adultery because she's been seen entering an "enclosed space" with a man other than her husband. (Confirmed adulterers are handled in another section.) Talmudic rabbis debate, for instance, how long the woman and man must have been sequestered in order to presume they had sex. Their arguments suggest that in ancient times the preferred encounter may have been the "quickie." One rabbi says it's the amount of time it takes to circle a date tree, while another says it's the time it takes a woman to remove a wood chip from her teeth (there's an additional debate about how deeply said wood chip was wedged). The scholars at least have the good sense to dismiss the position of Ben Azzai, a second-century commentator who says that coitis lasts the time it takes to roast an egg. They point out that Ben Azzai himself never married and therefore wouldn't (or shouldn't) be acquainted with such matters.

Another story in the Talmud says that a man can divorce his wife if she burns his soup. The reason is, if he's willing to divorce his wife simply because she burned his soup, the couple must have bigger problems.

A heavyset man with a thick Yiddish accent who hangs out at the clubhouse tells me that a woman who has sex with a non-

Jew can never go home again, not even if her husband forgives her. One interpretation of this is that the woman enjoyed sex with an uncircumcised man so much that her husband will always pale by comparison. The heavyset man seems extremely excited about sharing this information with me. He begins going into heated detail about the different acts that can qualify as adultery, including a whole range of lesbian possibilities. When I run into him a second time, he volunteers to take me on a fact-finding mission to a strip club that's supposedly frequented by married Hasidic men. Instead I go look for some pretzels.

Someone else at the clubhouse e-mails me a story that's been circulating on the Internet about a married yeshiva student named "Ari" who has long admired "Chani," the wife of his Talmud-study partner. Ari finally makes his move when his study partner goes off to a wedding in Toronto and Chani calls to see if he can fix a door in their bedroom. After a breathy buildup, Chani's long skirt comes off and Ari's *payos* go flying. When her "36DD" breasts come out, it's a moment of revelation. "Ari exhaled slowly. Wow! To think someone actually had this lady for a wife, seeing these beauties whenever he wanted! . . . He wondered how his [study partner] ever made it to yeshiva." By the time she calls to cancel her substitute-teaching job, with Ari "reverently caressing her aureoles," I'm kind of into it.

Not surprisingly, the encounter culminates in Chani giving Ari a blow job—the holy grail of Hasidic sex fantasies. When sociologist Hella Winston tells me about Hasidic men she's researched, I have a sudden intuition. "Why do I get the feeling this is all about blow jobs?" I ask her. "Yes, it's about blow jobs!" says Winston, author of a book on Hasidic rebels called *Unchosen*. Fellatio is so far into the realm of pure, nonprocreative pleasure that Hasidic men don't dare ask their wives to perform it. Though it involves the forbidden act of "spilling seed," it wouldn't qualify as adultery, so it seems less naughty than intercourse.

For most men this is probably just a fantasy. Hasidic men and women simply don't have many chances to cheat. They're scrutinized inside their communities, and they're like aliens outside them. The Hasidic world's most effective way of discouraging affairs isn't warning of divine punishment; it's closing off opportunities to cheat. In some sects women and unmarried men aren't allowed to have drivers' licenses, lest they drive themselves into temptation.

But perhaps the ultrachaste atmosphere simply calls more attention to the sex that's missing. One extramarital window of opportunity comes in the summertime, when wives and children retreat to country bungalows upstate, leaving the men behind to work and visit on weekends. I'm told that one rabbi insisted his followers arrange a midweek bus to the bungalows as well, depositing husbands there on Tuesday night after work and taking them back early the next morning. This "basically meant a sex bus—everyone smiled about it," a Satmar adherent tells me. "But the real reason is that the men are a little loose in the city, loose as in they can go to bars or, God forbid, cheat."

If cheating goes on between men and women who are both Hasidic, I didn't hear about it. One man told me he had a crush on an unmarried religious woman who worked in his office, but then she got married and left the company. The next time he spotted her on the street, she was "already half pregnant and she's wearing a wig" and had lost her allure. Meeting someone outside the religious world isn't a simple matter when you've got twelve-inch *payos* and your wardrobe consists of double-breasted black suits, white kneesocks, and a fourteen-hundred-dollar fur *shtreimel* hat. While I'm hanging around Brooklyn, a "gotcha" photograph circulates by e-mail of two middle-aged Hasidic men in what appears to be an average disco. I'm mostly struck by how out of place the men look. Both are at least a decade older than anyone else. And amid the crowd of fit twenty-somethings, their bulging waistlines conspicuously reflect a lifetime of being passed plates of noodle kugel.

These men aren't looking for extramarital love. They're like lusty teenagers suddenly let loose or Japanese *salarymen* out for a night of play. They seem to be living out a delayed and compressed version of the decade, their twenties, that they spent getting married and having babies. Perhaps they imagine that secular life is always like this. One of the men, who's wearing a black vest and sporting a bushy black beard, appears to be approximating a dance move with his fists clenched by his sides. The other, dressed almost identically, is clutching the bare back of a blonde in a pink halter dress. It's not clear whether she's going to turn around and slap him.

With these social graces, Hasidic men's best chance of getting that blow job is to pay for it. Some communities apparently look the other way as long as the men don't get their pictures plastered online. There's some very thin cover for this in Jewish law. Adultery per se is when a married woman has sex with a man other than her husband; a married man who cheats is committing a lesser sin. And the law technically allows a man to keep a concubine, as long as the concubine is unmarried and follows purity laws like not having sex for two weeks out of the month and immersing herself in a ritual bath called a *mikvah*.

These legal loopholes create a smoke screen for outings to bars, discos, and massage parlors. "It's always been prohibited and tolerated at the same time," Hella Winston tells me. "It's not like, 'Oh, you should go out and do this.' But it gets kind of excused." She and others mention that some Hasidic men ease their consciences by seeking out black prostitutes, who, though they might be impure, at least aren't Jewish. "All the women claim they're looking for a scholar—they say, 'He won't cheat on me,'" Winston says.

The sociologist William Helmreich, who studies Hasidim, says religious Jews tend to emphasize the commandments dealing with things people do alone—and are thus intended to signify their relationship with God. Adultery is something that's done between two people, and it's not specific to Judaism. "I think that's a major reason that adultery is more tolerated than eating pork chops," Helmreich says.

Even if a relationship meets all the legal requirements, few rabbis would be willing to publicly endorse keeping a concubine. Observant Jews don't just follow the letter of the law, and for every argument in the Talmud there's a counterargument, too. Abraham, the master of ceremonies at the clubhouse, takes me aside and tells me another story: "There were these two guys. One guy got the urge, so he found an unmarried woman, made sure she was not [impure]—she went to the woman's mikvah—and then he had relations with her. Then the next guy also had the urge, and he just went to bed with the first willing subject." How were the two men judged? "The rabbi threw the first one out of the school, because the first one planned it out. That premeditation was just too much. The second one, he was just human. What can you do?" The moral, he says, is "Just because you can't find chapter and verse that says it's *not* okay doesn't mean it *is* okay."

It's unclear how many Hasidic men really go to prostitutes. They're so conspicuous that a few black-hatted men spotted at a massage parlor probably make the phenomenon seem bigger than it is. However, there is evidently pent-up demand for extramarital action. In 1996 a man who identified himself only as "Yossi" papered religious neighborhoods in Brooklyn with flyers advertising a discreet matchmaking service. The service claimed to provide Orthodox men with proper concubines, who followed all the prescribed rituals. It's extremely doubtful that Yossi really had, as he claimed, any sex-starved "career women" lined up to bed Hasidim. But a *Washington Post* reporter confirmed that Yossi did indeed receive hundreds of calls from men who were interested in the service.

It's no wonder that they were curious. Shlomo, the groom who got those typed instructions on his wedding night, says that sex between him and his wife never picked up any steam, despite the fact that they went on to have seven children. Now in his forties, Shlomo is thin and languid, with a scraggly gray-and-brown beard and sky blue eyes. When he dangles a cigarette over his crossed legs, he looks like a Beat poet about to launch into verse. By contrast, his wife sounds like a square. After their wedding night, she refused to get naked again. When he brought home some religious books with advice for young couples, she studied them obsessively and tried to follow every directive to the letter.

"Let's do it!" Shlomo remembers telling her. "Even though you're Hasidic, you have to be like a woman!" Occasionally he pretended he had orgasmed before he actually did, so that she would relax. But that trick worked only a few times.

All of Shlomo's religious training failed to channel his sexual energy into his marriage. He started going to massage parlors and eventually graduated to full-on prostitutes. He bought blue jeans and hid his *payos,* hoping to seem like a regular guy. Finally he secretly rented an apartment. It wasn't just for sex, he says. It was also a place to escape from the constant gaze of the religious world. "It was enough for me to sit with a girl and watch movies," he says.

It's possible that Shlomo would have been a philandering husband even if he hadn't been religious. But being stranded in an unsexy, humorless marriage didn't help. Shlomo isn't a run-of-the-mill believer, but he isn't a loner either. He's sociable and at home in his own skin. He says his friends knew what he was up to and that some joined him. But it got to be a bit too public. People at a yeshiva near his secret apartment saw him walking with a woman in a short-sleeved shirt and short skirt. The gossip, like the e-mailed photos of the men in the disco, was irresistible. "They went to the rabbis and said, 'There's a Hasidic guy with a shiksa,'" he says, meaning a non-Jewish woman. "They called my family, like, 'You take care of it.'" When his wife's father and brother came to talk to him, they didn't warn him about the spiritual consequences of sinning. They threatened him with divorce, which could have separated him from his children and cut him off from the rest of his family.

MUSLIMS HAVE a different technique to keep believers from straying: polygamy. If a religious man can't stick to one wife, perhaps he can he stick to four?

I decide to see how this works in Indonesia, which has more Muslims than any other country. Less than twenty-four hours after arriving I'm in the Javanese city of Solo, sitting in front of Indonesia's self-declared polygamy king, Puspo Wardoyo. I'm prepared to hate him. Puspo, as everyone calls him, hosts a Polygamist of the Year competition and writes books on how others can replicate his success managing four wives (his range in age from twenty-five to forty). On the talk-show circuit, he tells enraged feminists that he's really out to help women by keeping their husbands away from prostitutes and broadening the pool of marriageable men.

Polygamy is legal here, but it has fallen out of favor. People under forty tell me that their grandfathers and even some of their fathers had multiple wives, but they don't know many people their own age who do. This change was the handiwork of General Suharto, who ruled Indonesia from 1967 to 1998. Suharto's government banned polygamy for civil servants and members of the military. Most middle-class families now treat a son's decision to take a second wife as a shameful secret, and educated women are embarrassed to settle for being second— though under the right circumstances some still do.

Although a minority of Indonesians practice polygamy, the fact that it's legal makes cheating easier to justify. Some 95 percent of Indonesians say religion is "very important" to them, making it the most religious country in Asia and one of the most religious in the world. Offices in modern high-rises have special prayer areas for employees, sometimes conveniently located right next to the lunchroom. A youth radio station I visit is decorated with posters of Western pop stars, but it rewards its top employee each year with an all-expenses-paid pilgrimage to Mecca.

Being very religious is a way to get status. In polls, more than half the population typically say Indonesia should replace its secular legal system with Islamic sharia law, though enthusiasm for sharia wanes when respondents are asked if they approve of specifics like cutting off thieves' hands and stoning convicted adulterers. Adultery is illegal, but it's handled by secular courts. The punishment is relatively mild: up to seven years in prison.

Puspo's unlikely pulpit to revive polygamy is a chain of fast-food chicken restaurants. He owns about forty of them all over

Indonesia. It's not immediately clear whether the polygamy campaign is a way to sell more chicken, or vice versa. It might not be the best marketing strategy. My friend who's come along to interpret tells me that her female friends in Jakarta refuse to eat in Puspo's restaurants.

Lesson number one: Polygamy is delicious. At Puspo's restaurant in Solo, where we meet for the interview, he orders us sizzling fried chicken and tofu with spicy peanut sauce, plus a special juice called "poligami" because it has four ingredients (Muslim men can have up to four wives).

Lesson number two: Polygamists are charming. I'm not sure why this surprises me, because by definition they attract lots of women. But I had expected Puspo, forty-seven, to seem menacing. In fact he has an appealing tanned face and the habit of grinning and looking straight into my eyes. In a country where you usually need to be rich already in order to get richer, he has a sympathetic rags-to-riches tale. He parlayed his parents' tiny chicken stand into the Wong Solo chain (Puspo himself is also known as "Wong Solo"). He says the business operates on Islamic principles, and that he donates some profits to charity.

Puspo's rationale for polygamy is all about adultery. He says that if wealthy married men like him don't take additional wives, they'll go to prostitutes or have affairs instead, which he says is sinful and "disgusting." "I recommend people have a clear conscience by taking that woman as a wife, instead of cheating," he tells me. Puspo insists, implausibly, that his four wives never argue. He does concede that the Islamic requirement that current wives approve of any additional ones is a sticking point.

Puspo also doesn't mention that Islam's original rationale for polygamy was to help women whose husbands had died in war. The prophet Mohammed married as many as thirteen women, most of whom were widows. (An exception was A'isha, who was about ten years old when they consummated their marriage.)

Puspo seems more intent on avoiding cellulite than aiding widows. He staged a pageant to select his fourth wife and decreed that contestants must be under twenty-five and weigh less than 121 pounds (skinny women have smaller vaginas and are easier to maneuver into certain sexual positions, he explains). No doubt Puspo is correct in saying that powerful men have a particular appeal in a country as poor as Indonesia: Three hundred fifty women showed up to compete in the first round.

The abundance of young, poor, beautiful women in Indonesia seems to be more significant than the Islamic prohibition on extramarital sex, known in Arabic as *zina*. "Most rich and successful people are cheating," Puspo says. "Most of my friends are cheaters. They cheat with prostitutes just for play." Their wives are powerless to stop them, he says. "When women are angry, men cheat more." If a wife divorces her husband because he's unfaithful, the next one will just cheat, too, he says.

But will four wives be enough, especially when the women are no longer young nymphs? For Puspo, having four wives has whetted his appetite for more. He tells me four isn't really the limit, since the prophet Mohammed himself had more. Speaking of which, he asks, do I happen to know an American woman who meets his requirements? (I'm disappointed to realize he has ruled me out on both age and weight grounds.)

When I tell him I'll give it some thought, he moves into a kind of psychic-seduction mode with my skinny interpreter. "I know your type," he says, gazing at her. "You're into loving someone even if he has two or three wives. It will take a lot of effort to persuade you that someone loves you." She is blushing so hard it takes her a minute to regain her composure and tell me what he's said. I jealously elbow back into the conversation by asking him what kind of man he thinks I would like. Puspo looks me up and down. "You like a strong, masculine man," he says. "You would like a guy like me."

THE MAIN HALL of central Jakarta's religious court is empty of people and practically of furnishings, except for a manual typewriter on a wooden desk and a chart on the wall showing cases tried during the current year. But seconds after I lean on the desk, since there are no chairs anywhere, a clerk rushes out to tell me to get off it.

The idea that men will cheat if they're not given the chance to have multiple wives isn't merely the view of one publicity-seeking entrepreneur. As I learn here, it's the quasi-official position, or at least the conventional wisdom.

Indonesia's religious courts handle family matters like births, deaths, and marriages. If someone wants to have a second, third, or fourth wife, he's supposed to register the marriage here. In addition to the standard Islamic requirement that husbands treat all their wives equally and get permission from a current wife to take on any others, Indonesian law adds the additional stricture that a man's current wife must be infertile, very sick, or unable to satisfy her husband in bed.

That's the letter of the law. But on a tour of the gilded court-room where cases are heard, the clerk says that sometimes a wife comes to complain that her husband has taken another wife without her permission. He says the court first looks into how wealthy the husband is and then investigates whether the first wife can fulfill him sexually. The clerk isn't clear about how this is determined, but simply reaching middle age is a strike against her. "A woman who's having menopause doesn't have any sexual desire, at the same time her husband still has strong sexual desire. That's the reason for having polygamy," he tells me.

I'm confused. How could the man have gotten married again without his first wife's permission? Another court official says that actually just one or two couples per year come in to register polygamous marriages, and according to the chart on the wall, so far this year none have done so. The second clerk explains. "There are two kinds of polygamy cases: Healthy ones who come here and ask permission from the court. And unhealthy—who don't register. There are many unhealthy cases." Last year the only case involved a Malaysian husband who disappeared in the middle of the proceedings. Perhaps someone pointed out to him that he was going through a need-less hassle.

Essentially, a man who wants to take second, third, or fourth wives doesn't bother registering those unions. He just sets up a house for the woman and starts having children. The other wife or wives are often the last to know. This court is where those wives would go to complain, which doesn't seem very promising.

The second clerk says even if a first wife proves that she's fertile, healthy, and can satisfy her husband in bed, the judge will probably rule in her husband's favor anyway. "Because if I don't give permission to the husband, the husband will continue to cheat in order to fulfill his desires," he says.

UNFORTUNATELY, there aren't any reliable sex statistics for Indonesia, or for most Muslim countries. Even researchers polling multiple countries tend to drop questions about sex from the surveys they use in the Muslim world. That means it's impossible to know the levels of infidelity in places like Iran, where convicted adulterers can be stoned to death. In Kazakhstan, where about half the population is Muslim, 1.6 percent of married or cohabiting men and 0.9 percent of women said they'd had more than one partner in the last year, according to a survey done in 1999. In Nigeria, which is also half Muslim, the figures were 15.2 percent for men and 0.6 percent for women, according to a survey from 2003.

Despite the lack of hard data, I'm starting to get the message that a lot of cheating goes on in certain circles in Indonesia, and that this is an open secret. The middle-class women and men I meet consistently tell me that adultery is absolutely wrong because the Koran forbids it. But in the next breath, many say it's actually quite common and that plenty of their friends are involved in extramarital relationships.

"Islam is not permissive," says Paulus Wirutomo, who heads the sociology department at the University of Indonesia. "But there's an emphasis on formality." While a religious ethos doesn't seem to prevent affairs, it does shape the sexual culture. Several people tell me they're discreet about cheating, because they don't want to do something that's a direct affront to Islam.

Polygamy legitimizes the idea that one woman isn't enough and effectively gives married men permission to date, sometimes even if they have no plans to convert their mistresses into wives. "Polygamy is something that induces adultery, in that before they get married for the second time, there's a period of adultery," Wirutomo tells me. Even highly educated women giggle nervously when I mention polygamy. They're always haunted by the possibility that their husbands will broach the subject.

Indonesians are accustomed to a big gap between the stated rules and the way things really get done. Transparency International, an organization that measures corruption around the world, ranks Indonesia as one of the most corrupt countries. Out of the 158 countries it covers, only about 21 are more corrupt.

There's even sympathetic local lingo for no-strings affairs. A *bobok bobok siang,* or BBS, is baby-talk slang for an "afternoon nap." A brief love affair is a *selingkuh,* which translates to a "wonderful interval." In these relationships both parties know that their marriages won't be affected.

Women get to enjoy these, too. One is Ria, a twenty-four-year-old woman in Jakarta who wears a white silk veil over her olive skin. Ria has a three-year-old son, a husband who makes a nice living, and a lover with whom she sleeps once a week and text-messages at least ten times a day.

"Look at me! I am a Muslim, I wear this veil. But I have another life," she says, clasping her head. She holds out her hands and shows me her rings: The diamond is from her husband, and (though her husband doesn't know it) the gold band is from her lover. Ria's parents are devout and phone her every day. They'd be furious if they found out she was cheating. But she relies on her lover, who's not married and lives nearby, for the kind of intimacy that her husband won't ever give her. Their marriage is more formal. Her husband is willing to pay for her to go back to school, but it's her lover who tells her she's smart and will succeed in a new career. "I still love my husband, but I need someone else to make me alive," she says.

Ria says many of her friends also have a respectable husband and then a younger and often unmarried lover on the side. She arranges for me to meet one of them, Dian, the next morning, in an almost-deserted mall. Dian, twenty-nine, says she took a lover after learning that her husband was seeing an old girlfriend. He argued that it was harmless and "only for fun."

Dian has a law degree, but her husband forbids her from working so that she'll be home when he gets back from work. She packs his briefcase in the morning, and if she forgets something, he calls from the office to chastise her. "I feel guilty, and I feel this kind of relationship is wrong, but I cannot change the reality that I need someone else. I feel very, very lonely," she says. "My lover can give me lots of attention while my husband is busy. He asks me if I've already had lunch or not. My husband never does that."

These restless housewives are easy pickings for foreign men, who are removed from the women's social networks and have an exotic appeal. Mike, an American in his late twenties who is in Jakarta doing academic research, has made a sport of bedding married women. He stopped pursuing single women after one of them text-messaged him the day after what he thought was a one-night stand to say that she wanted to have his baby.

"In the States I was just a normal dude who slept with girls, but not that much," Mike says. "It's so basic here, there's no game. You say, *'Mau kenal.'* It means 'I want to get to know you.' That's, like, flattering enough." His biggest complaint is that even married women typically wait until about the fifth meeting to sleep with him, their one concession to "appearances." After the sexual relationship has run its course, they say, "Thank you for the orgasm," and disappear, Mike says. A friend of Mike's, a New Zealander who's been in Indonesia for years, tells me that flings with married women very rarely convert to serious relationships. "Upsetting the order of things in Indonesia is not a good thing," he explained.

I'm skeptical that it's really so easy, so Mike lets me tag along with him to his favorite pickup spot. It's near the cosmetics counters in the front of a mall called the Blok M Plaza, where wealthy women peer through the glass to see if their drivers have arrived to collect them. When we arrive, I suggest a few women, but Mike immediately dismisses them as too young and thus potential "leeches." It takes only a few minutes for him to spot a suitable target. She's a thin woman with waist-length black hair, tight jeans, and a Brazilian soccer T-shirt. She's no older than twenty-five, with a giant engagement ring on her finger. Mike approaches her while I stay in the background snapping pictures. Literally minutes after he's started talking to her, they've both taken out their cell phones and are programming in each other's numbers.

Perhaps she had something more innocent in mind? I wonder.

Mike smiles patiently at me. "When a guy like me goes up to a girl like that and asks for her number, it's only for one thing."

Some foreign men get in deeper than they had planned. In Solo I meet a thirty-three-year-old Italian named Roman who has acquired four wives and sired twelve children, two of whom were born in the last two weeks. Like Puspo, he is a charmer; he has puppy-dog brown eyes and a full head of curly brown hair. Unlike Puspo, he is not in the publicity business and doesn't insist that all is well between his wives. "They hate each other. My life is hell," he tells me over whiskey at a bar near one of his four houses. "I don't understand why they cannot live all together."

Roman's wives range in age from twenty to twenty-two. Two have university degrees, and the other two finished high school. "After the third one, I didn't want to get married again," he tells me. "Here you marry the girlfriend and the whole family. You just give them [all] money." He converted to Islam last year to make everything proper. Each time he adds a new wife, the existing ones threaten to kill themselves. He earns enough manufacturing and exporting wooden furniture to afford the roughly six hundred dollars a month that each household costs. He lives alone but nevertheless gets calls at four in the morning from a wife demanding to know where he is and whom he's with. At least his parents are proud of him, he says.

Roman seeks solace from this chaotic life with a series of girlfriends, one of whom sends him a text message while we're speaking that says, "I'm telling you, someone's missing you a lot." The message is in English, because Roman doesn't speak Indonesian.

"I'm not very strong. I'm very weak. I cannot resist temptation," he says. He looks so sweet that I almost sympathize.

THERE'S A JOKE that's told about the handing down of the Ten Commandments on Mount Sinai. Moses comes down from the mountain and tells the Israelites, "There's good news and bad news. The good news is, I kept Him down to ten. The bad news is, adultery's still in there."

Every monotheistic religion, as soon as it gets going, immediately bans adultery. But I haven't seen any evidence that being religious keeps people from cheating. An American study done in 2001 found that among people who rated their marriages as "pretty happy" or "not too happy," even going to religious services two or more times a week barely affected whether they'd had extramarital sex. For all those hours in church to matter much, they had to already be in a "very happy" marriage.

Another study published in 2000 found that men who went to church regularly had fewer affairs than men who didn't. But among women, church attendance made no difference. Pastors themselves have an excellent opportunity structure for affairs, since they frequently do one-on-one counseling with members of their congregations. Dave Carder, an evangelical pastor based in Fullerton, California, decided to write a self-help book on adultery after two of the pastors he worked for ran off with congregants. Four members of a support group I visit in Memphis, for people with cheating spouses, are married to pastors.

Being religious can certainly make people feel more guilty about adultery. It calls the power of their faith into question. Some Christians in America have created a convenient way to explain their extramarital slips: They can't help it because they're addicted to sex. LIFE Ministries, based in Lake Mary, Florida, claims to have more than a hundred support groups across America for sex addicts and their spouses. The group, whose name stands for "living in freedom everyday," says addicts start with the "seemingly harmless" act of masturbation, then upgrade to Internet sex, fantasizing, and visits to strip clubs and prostitutes. At meetings, members pray and do exercises from the LIFE Ministries workbook. The director of a LIFE group in Florida tells me one of the oft-repeated messages is, "My body belongs to my wife, not to anybody else."

On topics where the Bible isn't clear, he says members use their own litmus test. "We tend to ask, would Jesus do that? Would He self-stimulate Himself? I don't think so."

Internationally, it's hard to find any correlation between religiosity and cheating. The French and the British are much less religious than Americans, but all three have similar levels of infidelity. Sub-Saharan Africans are among the most religious people in the world; in many countries in that region, over 80 percent of people say religion is "very important" to them. And yet Africa is probably the continent with the highest percentage of unfaithful men. Latin Americans also tend to be religious, and they cheat quite a lot, too.

Islam and Judaism, both of whose legal traditions make the American tax code look simple, also have the benefit of loopholes that seem to justify extramarital sex. In Indonesia the mere fact that polygamy is possible gives some men license to have girlfriends. Some religious Jewish men find arcane laws permitting them to keep concubines. Ironically, having a lot of laws—instead of just a broad moral code—may make it easier to commit adultery and still feel you're not sinning.

Ultimately, location trumps religion. Religious Christians in America behave more like other Americans than like Christians in other countries. Likewise, Indonesia's sexual culture is shaped as much by the fact that the country is poor as by the fact that it's highly religious. Whether Brazilians cheat or not depends as much on whether they live in the wealthier, less adulterous south or in the poorer, sexually rampant north as on how pious they are.

The Hasidim in Brooklyn intuitively understand the risk of fading into the mores of the country they live in. That's why some ban television sets. But setting up your tiny community as an island of purity in a sea of decadence is a dangerous thing. People get curious. And because they have to creep into the secular world furtively, they tend to end up in its tawdriest places.

Not a single religious person in any country told me he or she was afraid of divine retribution for cheating. Some didn't seem to feel guilty about it all. But the ones who did feel guilt all said they feared the opinions of their husbands, parents, pastors, or friends. Just as disease in South Africa is a distant and theoretical specter, so is God. If you want to know whether a person is likely to cheat, don't bother asking about his religious affiliation; ask for his passport and meet his friends.

The next and final stop on my world tour is China. It's often said that China's economic boom has brought a sexual revolution. I want to see if that means an explosion in adultery.

~~~~~

a sexual revolution

SOUTH AFRICANS WOULD rather die than be monogamous. And plenty of devout Muslims, Christians, and Jews prefer to risk the wrath of God than to stick to one partner. In
short, neither fear of death nor fear of God is enough to change
a sexual culture.

So what about money? What happens when in a very short
time, in the space of people's sexual lifetimes, a country goes
from being a poor and isolated place to having a thriving market economy? Do people change their sexual behavior? And if
they do, how do they justify it to themselves? And what about
those who get left behind?

I'm pondering these questions at the Lo Wu border crossing
between Hong Kong and mainland China at eight o'clock on a
Wednesday night. Surrounding me are throngs of men who are
also waiting to enter Shenzhen, the Chinese metropolis on the

other side of the border. Plenty of Hong Kongers work in Shenzhen, but most of these men tonight are traveling for pleasure. They've changed from their work clothes into shorts and sandals, and many are with friends. Another commuter train full of men pulls up to the border every five minutes.

These clerks, plumbers, and bus drivers are willing to brave the heat and the lines—not to mention the wrath of their wives and possibly the law—because just across the border in Shenzhen there is a siren's island of young women. For every man in line here, there are women in Shenzhen waiting to do whatever he wants, and a few things he might not have imagined.

Shenzhen is a utopia for adultery. Anyone who just wants a night of fun can choose from among plenty of prostitutes. But the city is also peppered with what local media have dubbed "second-wife villages." These are neighborhoods where women kept by their Hong Kong "husbands" supposedly pass their days playing mah-jongg, carrying around little dogs, and toting "real Louis Vuitton bags" (Shenzhen is also famous for its designer knockoffs). One Hong Kong woman, herself a former mistress, told me enviously that Shenzhen's second wives— known as *yi lai*—all have hourglass figures. The illegitimate children of liaisons between men from Hong Kong and women from Shenzhen are said to number at least half a million.

Hoping to appeal to the men's consciences, one Chinese legislator suggested plastering the Hong Kong side of the border with billboards that read YOUR CHILDREN ARE WAITING FOR YOU AT HOME. If Hong Kong husbands are having second thoughts, it's not immediately obvious, however. "Shenzhen women are cheap, beautiful, and young compared to Hong Kong girls," says Martin, forty-one, a handyman in Hong Kong who has a wife but stays with his *yi lai* four or five nights a week. "But the main point is that they're cheap." (Like many Hong Kong Chinese, Martin has both an English and a Chinese name.)

It's no accident that Shenzhen is ground zero for second wives. In the early 1980s, it became one of the first Chinese cities to welcome foreign investment. At the time Shenzhen was a fishing village with thirty thousand inhabitants. As foreign companies began opening factories and job seekers flooded in from China's poor interior, the population swelled. By 2005 it was home to 4.5 million people, most of whom had been born elsewhere. New arrivals, especially the pretty ones, soon figured out that they could earn much more in massage parlors and karaoke bars than assembling computers. Before they knew it, their patrons from both Hong Kong and mainland China were putting them up in apartments and paying for their groceries.

TO APPRECIATE HOW radical this new sexual landscape is, it helps to know how things used to be. In China's late imperial period, which lasted until the early twentieth century, a man was allowed only one wife but was by no means supposed to be sexually faithful to her. He could keep concubines and visit prostitutes whenever he liked. A wife, however, had just one sex partner for life: her husband. According to the historian Lisa Tran, he could banish or even kill her if she had sex with someone else.

Things changed in the early 1900s when China switched to a representative government, which professed to make men and women equal. Around the same time, public opinion was shifting to the idea that married men should be sexually faithful, too. Legislators and the public debated the issue for decades. Despite the legal arguments (weren't concubines really just wives?), men were reluctant to give up this privilege.

When the Communist Mao Zedong took power in 1949, he decided that concubinage was bigamy and therefore illegal. (Concubines remained legal in Hong Kong, which was ruled by Britain until 1997.) Prostitution was out, too. Mao decried promiscuity as "bourgeois" behavior, associated with rich men who indulged in selfish pleasures. He wanted to start fresh by putting everyone on an equal footing.

Mao's preoccupation with fidelity was emotional as much as practical. Authoritarian regimes like his assume that if they can penetrate the private realm of sex, they've got absolute control. Infidelity—the most secretive kind of sex—is their holy grail. In the Soviet Union, extramarital sex offered one of the few escape hatches. In George Orwell's *Nineteen Eighty-Four,* set in a fictitious totalitarian London, the main characters try to "escape" the party by having an extramarital affair (but later learn that the government was watching them all along).

In Maoist China adultery wasn't officially illegal, but it was ill-advised. Neighborhood committees—famously headed by hawk-eyed old women—kept watch over apartment buildings and reported anyone suspected of having "lifestyle problems" to party officials. Leaders of work groups could demote or even fire someone suspected of infidelity, or make the accused undergo a humiliating "self-criticism." Adulterous women, known as "broken shoes," were singled out for abuse. Affairs were so risky that people who had been sent away to work, with only a month of home leave every year, often preferred to suffer what became known as "sexual unemployment."

As in Soviet Russia, simply finding a place to cheat was a major hurdle. As late as 1988, the sociologists Zha Bo and Geng Wenxiu found that while Big Brother was no longer peeking through keyholes, "The crowded housing market remains unfavorable for affairs. It renders it difficult to become sexually involved outside of marriage without spouses, friends, colleagues or neighbors learning of it." According to their survey of city dwellers, spouses discovered the affairs of about 80 percent of cheating men and 87 percent of cheating women.

Romance was another casualty of Chinese Communism. During the Cultural Revolution, which lasted from 1966 to Mao's death in 1976, young city dwellers were plucked from their homes and sent away to work as peasants for years at a time. The most fervent work camps in the countryside explicitly banned "smoking and love." Some people married just to get a permit to come back to the city, and it was common to marry for "politics, economics and family background" rather than love, explain Zha and Geng. Matches frequently required approval from party bosses.

"To discuss any aspect of personal life, romantic relationships, or sex was considered bourgeois and hence taboo," Emily Honig writes in *Socialist Sex*. She quotes "sent-down" youth who recall that "all books about love were labeled pornographic, all songs about love labeled low-class. Men and women in love were considered hoodlums." One directive forbade Chinese from telling dirty jokes. People clandestinely circulated hand-copied romantic stories; the author of one such story was tracked down and imprisoned in 1975, for propagating "bourgeois love," Honig says.

Officials even purged any hints of sexual attraction from state-approved operas staged during that period. When male and female characters appeared together onstage, "they spoke only of work, the revolution, or class struggle, and they referred to each other as 'comrades,'" Honig says. It wasn't even clear to many people that Mao's accomplice in inciting the Cultural Revolution, Jiang Qing, was also his wife.

Mao didn't apply these strictures to himself. In a 1994 exposé, his longtime personal physician, Zhisui Li, writes that Mao's handlers were constantly procuring women who were "young, attractive and politically reliable" to satisfy the chairman's sexual appetites. Li says Mao favored virgins and compared himself to the Chinese emperors who kept thousands of concubines. After one dinner at a country villa, Mao holed up with his current mistress and her sister for three days, leaving them only for a meeting with the mayor of Shanghai.

"Asceticism was the public watchword of the Cultural

Revolution, but the more ascetic and moralistic the party's preachings, the further the chairman himself descended into hedonism," the doctor writes. "He was waited on constantly by a harem of young girls. It was at this time, the height of the Cultural Revolution, that Mao was sometimes in bed with three, four or even five women simultaneously." Among these women it was a mark of status to catch Mao's particular venereal disease.

When Mao died in 1976, he left behind a centralized economy. Reformers in his party took control, but to open China's economy they had to abandon some of the mechanisms they had used to patrol people's private lives. Bits of this happened by attrition: The hawkish old women got left behind when their entrepreneurial neighbors upgraded to luxury high-rises. Government work groups became irrelevant for yuppies.

More privacy, and more money, also created lots of little spaces where affairs could flourish. The *yi lai* is just one variety. China's new class of middle managers and professionals, who weren't interested in shacking up with poorly educated peasants, discovered each other in offices and at the dance halls that thrived in big cities like Shanghai. Restaurants and hotel rooms—the bread and butter of affairs—were suddenly within reach of people who also had the privacy and leisure time to "look for a direction." For those who were too shy to approach someone face-to-face or get tangled in office politics, the Internet was a godsend.

Although cheaters in China sometimes look to the past to

justify their behavior, there's a lot about Chinese adultery that's indisputably modern. For starters there's the nomenclature. "One-night love" in Chinese suggests a quickie encounter between white-collar workers who met in a Western-style bar or disco. "Net love" and "Internet lover" might involve only virtual meetings. "The fourth kind of feeling" implies a cocktail of the first three—friendship, love, and sex—which arises between men and women working for the same company. There's even a specific term for someone who tries to break up his lover's marriage.

All the new money coursing through China hasn't just enabled affairs. It has spawned an industry of infidelity, though, unlike the one in America, the Chinese version often encourages affairs. Matchmaking agencies pair visiting businessmen with local women. Sexologists and other new "experts" opine on the morality of extramarital sex on national talk shows. Popular soap operas dramatize affairs and play out the new moral scripts. Private detectives with agencies like Grand Shanghai Investigation spend most of their time hotfooting after suspected cheaters. (One well-known sleuth is known as "the mistress killer.") Several agencies are so successful they've franchised.

China is even exporting affairs. The super-rich eventually send their mistresses to graduate school in Australia rather than dumping them. Taiwanese newspapers have declared extramarital sex to be an "epidemic," in part because so many local businessmen are keeping mainland mistresses in the cities that they visit for work. A guide to keeping one's husband's pants zipped while he's on the road, *My Husband Is a Taiwanese Businessman in Mainland China,* was a best seller (although the author's own husband eventually ran off with his girlfriend). Taiwanese doctors reported a spike in vasectomies, supposedly at the request of wives who want at least to limit the damage from their husbands' dalliances.

MONEY HAS CREATED new opportunities for cheating in China. But money alone can't account for the fact that people are taking advantage of these opportunities. To enable them to do so, Chinese society had to agree on some new shared stories about when and with whom cheating is okay. People use these stories to justify their affairs to coworkers, to friends, and to themselves.

One of the new justifications is love—more specifically, the idea that cheating in the name of love isn't so bad, an excuse that will seem familiar to Westerners. Of course, Chinese have been falling in love for millennia. But, as the sociologist James Farrer points out, it wasn't until the late twentieth century that "romantic feelings" widely became something that was considered right to act on. By the early 1980s, popular magazines were debating whether it's better to divorce your spouse for a lover or stay in a loveless marriage, a discussion that would have been unthinkable just a few years earlier.

Educated urbanites were especially persuaded by the new

logic of romance. In the 1990 survey by Zha and Geng, 84 percent of men and 92 percent of women said married couples should be sexually faithful. But when the researchers asked if they would tolerate an affair "in pursuit of love," 40 percent of men and 28 percent of women who'd attended college said they would. (Less-educated people were less accepting.)

There isn't any firm proof that infidelity is on the rise in China. There were no meaningful sex surveys when Mao was in charge, to use as a point of comparison. But a nationally representative survey done in 2000, called the China Health and Family Life Survey, found that urban men, who are China's richest, were more promiscuous than China's overall population. Some 18.3 percent of urban men and 3.2 percent of urban women had cheated in the previous year, compared to 10.5 percent of men overall (there's no national figure for women yet). About 40 percent of people who sought a divorce in Shanghai in 2000 said they wanted to separate because of adultery. Divorce procedures, once forbiddingly cumbersome, now take about ten minutes and cost less than a Frappuccino.

China's economic boom has ignited the sexual appetites of the Hong Kongers next door. They didn't live through the most bitter years of Communism, since Hong Kong was under British rule until it was returned to China in 1997. But the flood of new money from China, which brought *yi lai* to the Hong Kong border, has attuned Hong Kong men to the ethos of romance, too. Martin, the forty-one-year-old Hong Kong handyman who waxes excitedly about how cheap it is to keep a *yi lai,* also takes pains to emphasize to me that he and his girl-friend, whom he met when she was eighteen, have strong feel-ings for each other. He describes their early meetings at the Shenzhen massage parlor as a kind of courtship. "I understood that she wanted it, too," he says of their decision to get an apartment together.

Having a "pure" romance may be even more important in a place where it seems as if money has infected everything. Mar-tin boasts several times that, unlike his real wife, his *yi lai* has never asked him for money. Martin points out that he comes from modest beginnings himself, so he and his *yi lai* have a shared "culture." "She prepares dinner and treats me like a king. She makes tea when I wake up. She lays out my clothes. You can't compare this to a Hong Kong wife. A Hong Kong wife wouldn't do this."

Martin thinks of his *yi lai* as a kind of concubine. Britain col-onized Hong Kong in 1842 but got around to banning concu-binage only in 1971 (it had been legal since the Qing dynasty). Concubines used to be a privilege of the rich, however. Now even working-class men like Martin can keep two households running.

But Martin's *yi lai* prefers to imagine herself as a proper wife. Martin says it's only the media and women in Hong Kong who use the expression *yi lai.* She tells her friends that Martin is single and insists that they call each other "husband" and "wife," even though she sits quietly when Martin's real wife calls his cell phone. (He tells his real wife that he's working the night shift.) "If I call her my *yi lai*, she'll think I'm insulting her. She accepts that I have another wife in Hong Kong. But in China I treat her like a wife."

When Martin arrives in Shenzhen, she shadows him to fend off other girls. (Like a real husband, he often arrives with friends a few hours before he's told her he's coming, so he can "play.") Martin boasts that he even told her his real name, unlike other Hong Kong men, who, he says, want to have the freedom to disappear when they lose their jobs or find younger girls. After four and a half years together, Martin and his *yi lai* have even written a romantic end to their story: Eventually she will get married, but she'll come back and "visit" him.

Saying your *yi lai* is with you purely for love is a bit like claiming your maid is part of the family. Try stopping her pay and see how long she sticks around. Farrer and his co-researcher Sun Zhongxin, who interviewed Shanghai residents about their affairs, found that people were so eager to have moral cover that they used the "romance" excuse regardless of what their deeper motives were. When the romantic spell shattered, money quickly bobbed to the surface. After a thirty-year-old single woman named Mimi found out that her Taiwanese lover wasn't going to leave his wife, she began demanding money from him. She also became aggressive. When his wife phoned the company where both Mimi and her lover worked and said, "This is Mrs. Li in Taipei," Mimi replied, "This is Mrs. Li in Shanghai."

Stories change depending on the circumstances. The same person who pleads romance might, when the subject of his wife comes up, rely on an older story: that a man who puts food on the table doesn't have to be faithful. "All men who keep mistresses will say they're responsible husbands and fathers. They will say, 'We bring the money home,'" the anthropologist Siumi Maria Tam at the Chinese University of Hong Kong tells me. "Money is an important indication of being a good husband. The emotional thing is very recent. . . . The easiest way to show that you're responsible is to bring money home and give money to parents."

China's sexual revolution is very contagious. I keep hearing stories about married Western men who, after working in China for a few months, decide that monogamy really isn't for them. Peer pressure shapes a sexual culture. When everyone around you is saying that cheating is normal, and that you're entitled to indulge yourself and no harm will come of it, it starts to sound like a good idea. Martin didn't decide to keep a *yi lai* just because he could afford it. His friends were doing it, too. In Shenzhen, he often goes out on group dates with other Hong Kong patrons, each with his own *yi lai*.

Affairs that manage to blend romance with financial gain have an epic quality in modern China. The patron saint of this maneuver is Wendi Deng, who elbowed her way into a series of opportunities that ended with the biggest catch: Australian billionaire Rupert Murdoch. The road to her marriage reads like an instruction manual for ambitious Chinese girls. According to the *Wall Street Journal,* Deng, the daughter of a factory director, was a sixteen-year-old student at Guangzhou Medical College when she met a California woman, Joyce Cherry, who offered to tutor her in English. The woman's husband, Jake, was helping the Chinese build freezers for factories. The couple was so taken with Deng that when she said she wanted to study in America, they sponsored her student visa and helped her apply to a college near their house. They even put her up until she could manage on her own. (Both Cherrys had by then moved back to California.)

Before long, Mrs. Cherry discovered alluring pictures that her husband had taken of Deng in a Chinese hotel room. Two years later the Cherrys were divorced, and Jake and Deng were married. According to the *Journal,* the marriage lasted just a bit longer than it took for Deng to get her American residency. Deng finished college and attended Yale's business school, then landed an internship and eventually a job in Hong Kong with Murdoch's Asian satellite service, Star TV. The *Journal* reports that just nine months or so after Deng first appeared in public as Murdoch's Chinese translator, Murdoch told company executives that their relationship was "serious." A year later Murdoch was divorced, and he and Deng were married.

Stories like this are a beacon to Chinese women of a certain social rank. Tam at the Chinese University of Hong Kong says, "Ask any undergraduate woman, 'What's your life goal?' 'Oh, to marry a rich guy.'"

NOT EVERYONE is caught up in China's new sexual culture. Many government officials would prefer to turn back the sexual clock to about 1970. The thought of millions of their constituents squirming around in the wrong beds makes the authorities in Beijing anxious. If for middle-class Chinese having affairs symbolizes the freedom and self-expression they've gained, for the government it embodies the control it has lost.

Beijing's unease periodically bubbles to the surface, as when a functionary declared that infidelity is destroying family values and raising the murder rate. Affairs are a convenient scapegoat for just about anything, and the topic diverts attention from more pressing issues, like the huge income gap between people in the countryside and those in cities.

Another supposed by-product of infidelity is corruption within the government's own ranks. A panel of experts determined that 95 percent of officials convicted of graft also had mistresses and that in the southern region (which includes Shenzhen) all of them did. The solution to corruption, the experts conclude, is to do away with affairs. The perhaps-convoluted logic is that officials go crooked to meet their mistresses' demands for expensive holidays and designer shoes, so if they don't cheat, they won't have to steal.

Occasionally an official body takes action against infidelity. The city of Nanjing ordered all city officials to report their mistresses to local authorities. Guangdong province, where Shenzhen is, passed a regulation to punish unmarried couples who live together with as much as two years in a labor camp. The law is aimed at married men and their mainland girlfriends. But few cases have been prosecuted, because the men's wives would have to bring charges, and they live in Hong Kong, which is a different jurisdiction.

At one point there was an earnest national debate—perhaps one of China's most open and democratic—about whether Beijing should criminalize adultery, what kinds of encounters count as affairs, and whether third parties should be prosecuted. There was even talk of making it illegal for married people to live apart. But the thought of much of the Chinese police force being diverted to stake out motel rooms sobered up the Communist rulers. The final version of the marriage law merely lets a person sue for damages in a divorce case if he or she can prove that a spouse is living with someone else.

Just as China's new sexual culture irritates the regime, it also offers nothing to the husbands and wives of people who are having affairs. They were happy with the old system, which protected their marriages.

Meeting Winnie, a Hong Kong seamstress in her fifties who was born on the mainland and came to Hong Kong only when she was twenty, reminds me that China may be the worst place on earth to be a middle-aged woman. Winnie got her first inkling that things were changing in her marriage when her husband began taunting her about other women. "He said, 'If I find a woman who is uglier than you, what do you think? If I find a woman who is as pretty as Lee Ka Yan [a former Miss Hong Kong], what do you think?'" Winnie was sad. She has thick arms and a flat face. She would not be mistaken for Lee Ka Yan.

Her husband had been spending a lot of time back in the Chinese city two hours from Hong Kong where they are both from, supposedly to help a friend find a wife. And something had gotten to him there. He didn't want to spend Saturdays with Winnie and their daughter anymore. His mind was someplace else.

When Winnie and her husband were on a trip to their hometown, two young women came into a restaurant where they were eating. The women sat at a nearby table but didn't speak. One of them looked a lot like Lee Ka Yan. Winnie felt that it was a test, or a viewing. When she asked her husband about the incident the next day, he said he didn't remember seeing the women.

In fact, he wouldn't tell her anything about what was going on, perhaps because none of his stories would stand up to her scrutiny. But when she called his company, his colleagues thought she was the other woman. "They said, 'Oh, you're in Hong Kong from China.' Everyone knew about the woman, but I didn't." Her husband still wouldn't directly admit to anything, but he would occasionally say, "It's not a problem because everyone does this."

Winnie was desperate. She reached for a story that was somewhat familiar to her. "I told my husband, 'If you need two women, then I am the bigger wife. . . . The smaller wife should bring *me* a cup of tea.'" But there was no tea. Her husband was immersed in a different narrative, one backed up by his friends and work colleagues. And it didn't involve giving special status to his wife. "I think he was so proud of himself for having two women," she says.

Winnie wasn't part of China's new sexual culture, and she didn't believe in divorce. But because she was out of her depth, and flailing, she threatened to divorce her husband if he didn't stop seeing the other woman. He knew that the threat wasn't meant to be taken literally, but it was just the opening he needed, to avoid being a husband who technically dumped his wife. Winnie still seems shocked that she's a divorcée. And she's ready to forgive her husband if he'll just come home. "The Chinese saying is, 'When you marry a chicken, you need to follow the chicken. When you marry a dog, you need to follow the dog.'"

The sexual culture in China has changed more radically, and more quickly, than in any other place I visited. People don't just have more money now. They also expect a kind of personal fulfillment that was hard to imagine a few decades ago. It's not surprising that marriages made in another era can't survive in this one. And while there aren't any long-term statistics, the circumstantial evidence suggests that there's a lot more cheating going on. Not only are there so many more opportunities to cheat, but Chinese society has given itself permission to take advantage of them.

WHEN I CROSS the border into Shenzhen, I'm still depressed from my meeting with Winnie. I want to see what all the fuss is about.

A twenty-minute taxi ride later, my companion (a Hong Kong man who's offered to act as my unofficial tour guide and interpreter) and I are in a second-wife village. And though it's in the center of a metropolis, I can see why it's called a village.

The buildings are all low. People are walking down the middle of the streets. And everywhere, everywhere, there are young women, some probably still in their teens. If I didn't know better, I'd think I was in student housing during summer break. Women are sitting inside storefronts or on folding chairs in front of makeshift restaurants. They're dressed casually. It takes me a minute to register the expression on many of their faces: boredom. There are lots of little streets, some more like alleyways, and this same scene of bored women on folding chairs keeps repeating itself. My companion has to remind me that all of the women either are for sale or have already been bought.

We walk around for a while until I realize that my companion has a destination in mind: a massage parlor. We arrive at one he seems familiar with; there are women out front holding clipboards and wearing long satin dresses. I'm reluctant to go inside. The thought of all the fluids that are exchanged here makes me regret wearing sandals instead of covered shoes.

We pass go. To my surprise, it is extremely clean. Girls (I need to call them that, because they're so young) in pink satin jodhpurs and ponytails scamper around. My companion confers with a hostess, who leads us into a large room with a giant flat-screen television and a bank of cushioned chairs set above tubs of warm water for our feet. It's a cross between a disco and a pedicure salon. I remind myself that I am here for the purpose of doing research and that places like this are the source of Winnie's suffering.

Then I hear the price of the foot massage we're about to receive: $3.50 for eighty minutes. This includes tea and cool slices of watermelon. I slide into one of the soft chairs. A girl in pink jodhpurs approaches me and begins rubbing my temples (a "foot" massage starts with the head here). My thoughts of Winnie, and of catching hepatitis, ebb away. I wonder if I can buy another massage after this one. And I'm thinking I might come back to Shenzhen.

home sweet home

AFTER WANDERING AROUND the world to see how people cheat, I'm finally back at my desk in Paris. My world ranking of adultery is pinned to the wall next to me, like a talisman. It gives me the illusion that I have a handle on this vast, slippery, and possibly unknowable topic.

I've discovered that some of the stereotypes Americans hold about foreigners are wildly outdated. I'd always heard that Italian men are world-class philanderers. In fact, they commit less adultery than American men—which is to say, they don't cheat very much. That stereotype about Italians may have contained some truth between 1880 and 1920, when millions of Italians emigrated to America and brought their stories about Italy with them. But it's not true of modern Italy.

Many such stereotypes endure from other eras. I grew up hearing about fog in London; in fact, it was smog, which was all but eradicated by Britain's Clean Air Act of 1956. American soldiers returned from World War II with tales of Frenchwomen who didn't shave their armpits and hid their body odor with copious amounts of perfume. Stories of French promiscuity had been legion for centuries. In fact, Paris is now home to some of the cleanest and best-epilated women in the world. And contemporary Frenchmen cheat about as much as Americans.

We Americans even cling to false notions about ourselves. Americans persist in believing dubious statistics from the 1940s and 1950s suggesting that cheating is very prevalent. Some Americans even take a sly satisfaction in the idea that women now manage to schedule extramarital trysts in between their sales presentations and parent-teacher conferences. This is taken as evidence of increasing equality between the sexes.

In fact, as I learned, Americans don't cheat much. In 2004, just 16 percent said they had ever been unfaithful to a spouse, and only 3.5 percent said they'd cheated in the last year. There's no firm evidence that more women are cheating now, despite the fact that more go to work. Sex statistics surely aren't a perfect representation of how people behave, but it's telling that the levels of infidelity in America have remained fairly steady through the last eleven national surveys, conducted over a period of sixteen years.

Although Americans believe that cheating is common, our expectations of marriage have risen so much that we have trouble believing our own spouse would ever be unfaithful. When we discover that a partner has strayed, it's so world-shattering that we head into a kind of post-traumatic stupor. This comes with its own contradictions. I get the sense that Americans sometimes take a certain satisfaction in all the drama that affairs create. Being a "betrayed spouse" is an identity and, for some, even a vocation.

Americans weren't always so willfully naïve about affairs. Women of my grandmother's generation didn't usually fret about whether their marriages were personally fulfilling or not. But since it became much easier to divorce in the 1960s, we've been holding our marriages—and our lives—to an extremely high standard. We strive for perfect health and fitness, and we expect emotionally satisfying marriages and complete fidelity.

In America, marriage is even supposed to resolve one's existential angst. A married person doesn't have to worry whether she's fundamentally alone and unknowable. She's *married*. There's at least one person with whom she has no barriers and no secrets. Religious Americans invoke the biblical expression that they and their spouses are "one flesh." Though previous generations may have been more sanguine about the challenges of monogamy, nowadays any slip is—at least theoretically— grounds for divorce. Adultery robs us of the happy ending that we believe—despite all the evidence to the contrary—is our due.

This outsize preoccupation with monogamy doesn't seem to do Americans much good. We cheat in roughly the same proportion as many of those foreigners who are calmer about infidelity. Our high expectations for personal happiness might even make us more likely to cheat. After all, aren't we entitled to an affair, if that's what it takes to be fulfilled?

When Americans do cheat, it gets very messy. Despite the existence of our vast marriage-industrial complex, adultery crises in America last longer, cost more, and seem to inflict more emotional torture than they do in anyplace else I visited. The discovery of an affair is so calamitous that on adultery Web sites people use war terminology to describe it: D-day. Polls show that Americans who have cheated are less likely to describe themselves as "very happy" than those who haven't (although it's not clear if infidelity is the cause or the effect).

Americans are such poor cheaters that we're even prone to suffer during the act of extramarital sex. I didn't find any other country whose citizens get naked with their lovers but specifically don't have intercourse, so that they can semitruthfully tell themselves and their spouses that they didn't have sex. There's almost certainly no other country where adulterers routinely insist that they're not the cheating type. What's the point of having a secret love affair if you're going to spend most of it feeling guilty? And then, if you're discovered and you stay married, you face years of recriminations from your spouse, during which you may be called upon to create a time line of every anxiety-filled caress you exchanged with your lover. Divorce might come as a relief after that.

In America, affairs can escalate even if neither party really wants them to. Extramarital relationships are so stigmatized that lovers prefer to treat the affair as a relationship that is socially acceptable: a courtship that leads to marriage. An "other woman" who's single is almost obliged to aspire to the more respected role of "wife." I heard about people who left their marriages to be with their affair partners just so they wouldn't feel like such creeps.

One husband in his early forties was so eager to distance himself from his own behavior that he described entering an affair with a coworker as almost involuntary. "I actually really enjoyed just kind of talking with her; I didn't really want the relationship to move beyond where it was." The husband told me he didn't envision his weekly lunches with the woman moving into what he now calls, with distaste, "this sexual thing." Things escalated anyway. He didn't tell his wife when he and the woman went to a basketball game together, and then when they went for a stroll around the city.

His account of what happened next was fragmented and dreamlike. "She said, 'You know, we could get a room here,' and I just thought, 'Whoa, that's really scaring me.' I said, 'No,' and I really kind of declined the first few invitations for that sort of stuff. And then in reality she kind of wore me down. I really didn't want to, because, you know . . . whatever." When he got to the part about how he's really not the cheating type, I wanted to sock him.

Some Americans even have trouble admitting that adultery is appealing. Their advice is, "If you want to cheat, just get a divorce." What this doesn't acknowledge is that affairs can be exciting precisely because one is married. Sometimes we want to be bound *and* free. An affair has all the pleasure of an intense courtship without any of the anxiety about how it's going to end. In fact, the ending has already happened, but with someone else (the spouse).

Life isn't as neat as many Americans wish it would be. In Isaac Bashevis Singer's novel *Enemies, a Love Story,* the main character, a Polish-Jewish immigrant to America, grapples with three different women. He gets little sympathy from anyone in his adopted country. "American lawyers had simple solutions for everything: 'Which one do you love? Divorce the other one. End the affair. Find a job. Go to a psychoanalyst.'"

Though the juggling act is running him ragged, he can't bear to give up any of the women. "'I want to have all three, that's the shameful truth,' he admitted to himself. 'Tamara's become prettier, calmer, more interesting. She's suffered an even worse hell than Masha. Divorcing her would mean driving her to other men. As for love, these professionals used the word as if it were capable of clear definition—when no one had yet discovered its true meaning.'"

These days monogamy is the ideal almost everywhere, and people in wealthy, Western countries usually don't stray very much. But outside America, they tend to accept that it's normal for married people to have little crushes and attractions, and to sometimes act on these feelings. When they do, it doesn't automatically mean that the married couple has been, in the American parlance, living a lie for years. Adultery brings heartache everywhere, but context and expectations determine the strength of the heartache.

Perhaps we could take a lesson from the French. In general, when they have an affair, they give themselves permission to enjoy it. They plan nice meals, find romantic settings, and don't beat themselves up about what they're doing. And if they don't want the affair to escalate, it doesn't. One Parisian said his mistress reprimanded him for not following the rules for mistresses: He should buy her presents and take her away for the weekend at least once. If he follows these rules, she can tell her mother and her girlfriends about it. There will certainly be frustrations along the way, but those problems won't be compounded by a heavy social stigma and false expectations about where the relationship is headed.

I was amazed that some French people, and a few Japanese, never confronted their spouses for cheating. In the case of one Parisian couple, the affair eventually ended, the husband sensed that his wayward wife had returned emotionally to their marriage, and they seemed to be living in a state of reasonable contentment. The affair caused a difficult period, but this didn't erupt into a long and consuming crisis. I don't think I'd be capable of reacting to an infidelity with such composure. But I might be better off if I could.

There's something else that we could learn from pretty much any foreign country. The American idea that a husband and wife should reveal the entire contents of their brains to each other doesn't exist anywhere else. Doing so probably removes a necessary mystery from marriage. It might be better to have some secrets, or at least to pretend that you do.

Americans may finally be getting more realistic about infidelity. The latest crop of advice from experts is that married couples should discuss the distinct possibility that—shock!— each might one day be attracted to someone else. The couples are supposed to devise a strategy for what to do if this happens.

The experts reason that an affair can be averted if either party is allowed to come home from work and confess that he or she was invited out for lunch by a cute colleague, and that the offer was tempting. Removing the secret build-up supposedly makes an affair less enticing.

I doubt that any of the affair-busting techniques invented by America's marriage-industrial complex will dent the overall levels of infidelity here. It doesn't seem humanly possible for a society to cheat much less than we do. We're already near the bottom of the world adultery rankings. Just as economies have a certain level of structural unemployment, countries seem to have a minimum level of structural infidelity (around 3 percent of men are unfaithful in a given year). The only countries known to have dipped far below that level are Bangladesh and Kazakhstan, which have other problems.

Americans have the luxury of setting standards for marriage and fidelity that people in some other countries wouldn't dream of. In Diane Johnson's novel *Le Divorce,* a married Frenchman tells his young American lover, "Your founding fathers expressed a hope for the future and a commitment to preparing the conditions that would make possible the best outcomes. But somewhere along the way, hope was transubstantiated into belief incarnate. I believe you call it The Power of Positive Thinking. Of course French people have no such delusions that things will work out for the best." Most likely, we Americans will go on believing they will.

ACKNOWLEDGMENTS

To WRITE THIS BOOK, I depended on the kindness of strangers, many of whom have become friends. I would never have penetrated Japan without the help of Yoko Itamoto, Atsuko Imai, Maikiko Wakai, Etsuko Yaguchi, Tomoko Greer, Henry Atmore, Meryl Davies, and my interpreter, Maiko Sawada, who forged on through blisters and exhaustion.

For helping me to navigate in Russia, I'm indebted to Vladimir Soldatkin, John Varoli, Carla Davidovich, Simcha Fishbane, Lynn Visson, Tim Gadaski, and Michele Berdy. Thanks to Andrew Miller and Emma Bell for their hospitality in Moscow.

I received generous help in South Africa from Clifford Barnett, Yael and Darrel Kadish, Hillel Braude, Michael Brown, Isak Niehaus, and Robin Smalley of mothers2mothers, who even fetched me from the airport. Ntombi and Fuzi Dhlamini did research and led me on an unforgettable tour of Soweto.

For their help in France, I am grateful to Jonathan Shenfield, Martina Neumann, Simone Bateman, Alice Ferro, Adeline Escobar, and ace photographer Dietlind Lerner. Thanks to dear friends Nicole-Anne Boyer and Toby Paterson for many comforting meals between drafts.

D. Y. Suharya made my Indonesian journey possible and provided helpful suggestions on the text. Many thanks also to Adam Ellick, Noor Huda Ismail, and Douglas Griffin. For their help on the China chapter, I am grateful to Lobo Lo, Ada Chau, Karrie Ping Li, Anna Yuen at Caritas, and Lisa Tran.

My wisest friend also happens to be my brother, Ken; thanks to him for incisive comments and ideas all along the way. Hannah Kuper read the statistics chapter and joined me for a few cold days in Moscow. Adam Kuper opened doors in South Africa, was a top-notch reader, and gave me the best advice on writing: Take a bath.

Thanks to Marsha Wolfman and Henry Druckerman for opening their home and their Filofaxes to me, and to Bonnie Green for letting me convert her living room into an office. And thank you to my sweet grandmother Esther for predicting, decades ago, that I would one day write a book.

I got additional help in America from Peggy Vaughan, Betina Schonberger, Emily Wolfman, Jinx Silver, Yitzchak Schonfeld, Hella Winston, Jeffrey Sumber, Mali Sananikone Gaw, and Shana Hildebrand. David Smith at the New York Public Library not only helped me with research but did so with alacrity and good humor. Tom W. Smith at the National Opinion Research Center, Emma Slaymaker, Osmo Kontula, Nathalie Bajos, and Nathalie Beltzer all came to the rescue during my quest for statistics.

This book is better because of comments from Elisabeth Eaves, Chen-li Sung, Rana Mitter, Natacha Henry, Patrick Weil, Yaël Ginzburg, and Nancy Gelles. I am also extremely grateful to Jane Fleming, my editor at The Penguin Press. Special thanks go to the people whose early enthusiasm set this book in motion: Roger Lowenstein, Suzanne Gluck, Michael Wolff, and Carlos Lizarralde.

This book also would not have been possible without the many generous people who told me their stories of infidelity. My thanks to all of you, and especially to a certain couple in Memphis, Tennessee.

People sometimes compare writing a book to having a baby. Having now done both, almost simultaneously, I can say definitely that a book hurts much more. My thanks to Leila for remaining joyful through all those hours when I was looking at my laptop instead of at you.

Few men would propose marriage to a woman who's writing a book on adultery. Simon Kupor not only married me, he read every draft. For your intellectual bravery, your love, and your patience, I am forever grateful.

BIBLIOGRAPHY

BOOKS

Anderson, Nancy C. *Avoiding the Greener Grass Syndrome: How to Grow Affair-Proof Hedges Around Your Marriage.* Grand Rapids: Kregel Publications, 2004.

Buruma, Ian. *The Missionary and the Libertine: Love and War in East and West.* London: Faber and Faber Ltd., 1996.

Chirac, Bernadette, and Patrick de Carolis. *Conversation.* Paris: Plon, 2001.

Cott, Nancy F. *Public Vows: A History of Marriage and the Nation.* Cambridge, MA: Harvard University Press, 2000.

Draitser, Emil A. *Making War Not Love: Gender and Sexuality in Russian Humor.* New York: St. Martin's Press, 1999.

Duncombe, Jean, Kaeren Harrison, Graham Allan, and Dennis Marsden, eds. *The State of Affairs: Explorations in Infidelity and Commitment.* Mahwah, NJ: Lawrence Erlbaum Associates, 2004.

Ericksen, Julia A., and Sally A. Steffen. *Kiss and Tell: Surveying Sex in the Twentieth Century.* Cambridge, MA: Harvard University Press, 1999.

Goodwin, Jan. *Price of Honor.* New York: Plume, 1994.

Haavio-Mannila, Elina, Osmo Kontula, and Anna Rotkirch. *Sexual Lifestyles in the Twentieth Century: A Research Study.* Houndmills: Palgrave, 2002.

Jack, Andrew. *The French Exception.* London: Profile Books Ltd., 1999.

Johnson, Diane. *Le Divorce.* New York: Plume, 1997.

Kon, Igor S. *The Sexual Revolution in Russia.* Translated by James Riordan. New York: Free Press, 1995.

Laumann, Edward O., Stephen Ellingson, Jenna Mahay, Anthony Paik, and Yoosik Youm. *The Sexual Organization of the City.* Chicago: University of Chicago Press, 2004.

Leleu, Gerard. *La Fidélité et Le Couple.* Paris: Flammarion, 1999.

Li, Zhisui. *The Private Life of Chairman Mao: The Memoirs of Mao's Personal Physician.* Translated by Tai Hung-chao. London: Arrow Books, 1996.

Michael, Robert T., John H. Gagnon, Edward O. Laumann, and Gina Kolata. *Sex in America: A Definitive Survey.* New York: Little, Brown and Company, 1994.

Moskowitz, Eva S. *In Therapy We Trust: America's Obsession with Self-Fulfillment.* Baltimore: Johns Hopkins University Press, 2001.

Pingeot, Mazarine. *Bouche Cousue.* Paris: Editions Julliard, 2005.

Sauer, Derk. *Typisch Russisch.* Amsterdam: Veen, 2001.

Sinclair, Joan. *Pink Box: Inside Japan's Sex Clubs.* New York: Harry N. Abrams, Inc., 2006.

Singer, Isaac Bashevis. *Enemies, a Love Story.* New York: Farrar, Straus and Giroux, 1972.

Spira, Alfred, Nathalie Bajos, and the ACSG group. *Les Comportements Sexuels en France.* Paris: La Documentation Française, 1993.

Spring, Janis Abrahms, and Michael Spring. *After the Affair.* New York: Harper Perennial, 1997.

Tiersky, Ronald. *François Mitterrand: The Last French President.* New York: St. Martin's Press, 2000.

Walton, George Lincoln. *Why Worry?* Philadelphia: J. B. Lippincott, 1908.

ARTICLES

Ali, Lorraine, and Lisa Miller. "The Secret Lives of Wives." *Newsweek,* July 12, 2004.

Allen, Elizabeth S., David C. Atkins, Donald H. Baucom, Douglas K. Snyder, Kristina Coop Gordon, and Shirley P. Glass. "Intrapersonal, Interpersonal, and Contextual Factors in Engaging in and Responding to Extramarital Involvement." *Clinical Psychology: Science and Practice* 12, (June 2005): 101.

Alia, Josette. "L'infidélité au feminin." *Le Nouvel Observateur,* August 19, 1999.

Altman, Lawrence. "Rare Cancer Seen in 41 Homosexuals." *New York Times,* July 3, 1981.

Atkins, David C., Neil S. Jacobson, and Donald H. Baucom. "Understanding Infidelity: Correlates in a National Random Sample." *Journal of Family Psychology* 15, no. 4 (December 1, 2001).

Beattie, Alan. "What's the Damage?" *FT Magazine,* October 2, 2004.

Betzig, Laura. "Causes of Conjugal Dissolution: A Cross-Cultural Study." *Current Anthropology* 30, no. 5 (December 1989): 654–76.

Birenbaum, Guy, and Philippe Berti. "Nicolas Sarkozy Sous le Choc," *VSD,* August 31–September 6, 2005.

Blumenfeld, Laura. "The Oy of Sex: Adultery Can't Be Kosher. Can It? A Story About God, Conscience . . . and Concubines." *Washington Post,* June 2, 1996.

Bremner, Charles. "How Mitterrand's Secret Network Spied to Protect the President." *Times* (London), November 20, 2004.

Buss, David M., and Todd K. Shackelford. "Susceptibility to Infidelity in the First Year of Marriage." *Journal of Research in Personality* 31 (1997): 193–221.

Campbell, Matthew. "'Napoleon' Sarkozy Bars Wife's Biography." *Sunday Times* (London), November 20, 2005.

Carael, Michel John Cleland, Jean-Claude Deheneffe, Benoit Ferry, and Roger Ingham. "Sexual Behavior in Developing Countries: Implications for HIV Control." *AIDS* 9, no. 10 (October 1995): 1171–175.

Carr, Adam. "Behavior Change in Response to the HIV Epidemic: Some Analogies and Lessons from the Experience of the Gay Communities." Paper prepared in December 1991 for the United Nations Development Programme series of HIV and Development Programme Issues Papers.

Chang, Jui-Shan. "Scripting Extramarital Affairs: Marital Mores, Gender Politics, and Infidelity in Taiwan." *Modern China* 25, no. 1 (January 1999): 69–99.

Choi, Kyung-Hee, Joseph A. Catania, and M. Margaret Dolcini. "Extramarital Sex and HIV Risk Behavior among U.S. Adults." *American Journal of Public Health* 84 (1994): 2003–2007.

Delius, Peter, and Clive Glaser. "The Myths of Polygamy: A History of Extramarital and Multi-Partnership Sex in South Africa." *South African Historical Journal* 50 (2004): 84.

Didion, Joan. "Clinton Agonistes." *New York Review of Books* 45, no. 16 (October 22, 1998).

Douzet, Frederick. "Du Watergate au Monicagate." *Le Monde,* August 29, 1998.

Eberstadt, Nicholas. "Russia's Demographic Straightjacket." *SAIS Review* 24, no. 2 (Summer 2004): 9.

Epstein, Helen. "The Fidelity Fix." *New York Times Magazine,* June 13, 2004.

———. "The Mystery of AIDS in South Africa." *New York Review of Books* 47, no. 12 (July 20, 2000).

Farrer, James, and Sun Zhongxin. "Extramarital Love in Shanghai." *China Journal,* no. 50 (July 2003): 1–36.

Gagnon, John, Alain Giami, Stuart Michaels, and Patrick de Colomby. "A Comparative Study of the Couple in the Social Organization of Sexuality in France and the United States." *Journal of Sex Research* 38, no. 1 (February 2001): 24–34.

Glass, Shirley, and Thomas L. Wright. "Justifications for Extramarital

Relationship: The Association between Attitudes, Behaviors, and Gender." *Journal of Sex Research* 29, no 3 (August 1992): 361–87.

Gopnik, Adam. "C'est la Lie." *New Yorker,* February 9, 1998.

Greeley, Andrew. "Marital Infidelity." *Society* 31, no. 4 (1994): 9–13.

Grossman, Joanna. "Punishing Adultery in Virginia: A Cheating Husband's Guilty Plea Is a Reminder of the Continued Relevance of Adultery Statutes." Findlaw.com, December 16, 2003.

Haavio-Mannila, Elina, and Osmo Kontula. "Single and Double Sexual Standards in Finland, Estonia and St. Petersburg." *Journal of Sex Research* 40, no. 1 (February 2003).

Henley, John. "Chirac Shown as Serial Seducer." *Guardian,* September 19, 2001.

———. "Sarkozy Plans to Sue Media for Revealing Lover's Identity." *Guardian,* October 13, 2005.

Hill, Zelee E., John Cleland, and Mohamed M. Ali. "Religious Affiliation and Extramarital Sex among Men in Brazil." *International Family Planning Perspectives* 30, no. 1 (March 2004): 20–26.

Hoffman, Michael. "Marriage—the Beginning of the End." *Japan Times,* September 12, 2004.

Honig, Emily. "Socialist Sex: The Cultural Revolution Revisited." *Modern China* 29, no. 2, April 2003:153–75.

Hooper, Joseph. "Infidelity Comes Out of the Closet." *New York Times,* April 29, 1999.

Huret, Marie, and Delphine Saubaber. "Enquête sur l'Infidélité." *L'Express,* July 19, 2004.

Israel, Betsy. "The Crush." *More,* July–August 2004.

Iwakami, Yasumi. "Men's Dream." *Monthly Gendai,* July 2000.

Kon, Igor S. "Sexuality and Politics in Russia, 1700–2000," *Sexual Cultures in Europe: National Histories.* Franz X. Eder, Lesley Hall, and Gert Hekma, eds. Manchester, UK: Manchester University Press, 1999.

Kreider, Rose M. "Number, Timing and Duration of Marriages and Divorces: 2001," U.S. Census Bureau.

Landler, Mark. "For Hong Kong Men, Mistresses on the Mainland." *New York Times,* August 14, 2000.

Laumann, Edward O., Robert T. Michael, and John H. Gagnon. "A Political History of the National Sex Survey of Adults." *Family Planning Perspectives* 26, no. 1 (January–February 1994): 34–38.

Lauria, Lisa M. "Sexual Misconduct in Plymouth Colony," The Plymouth Colony Archive Project, University of Virginia, 1998. http://etext.virginia.edu/users/deetz/Plymouth/Laurial.html.

Lawrence, Jill, and Jessica Lee. "Leaders Call for Decorum in Congress." *USA Today,* September 10, 1998.

Lévy, Bernard-Henri. "In the Footsteps of Tocqueville (Part V)." *Atlantic Monthly,* November 2005.

Lhomeau, Jean Yves. "La Vie Privée du Chef de l'Etat et Alors?" *Le Monde,* November 4, 1994.

Lippman, John, Leslie Chang, and Robert Frank. "Rupert Murdoch's Wife Wendi Wields Influence at News Corp." *Wall Street Journal,* November 1, 2000.

Liu, Chien. "A Theory of Marital Sexual Life." *Journal of Marriage and Family* 62, no. 2 (May 2000): 363–74.

Mapes, Timothy. "Table for Five? Chicken Magnate Puts Polygamy on the Menu." *Wall Street Journal,* November 24, 2003.

McCallum, Jack, and George Dohrmann. "The Dark Side of a Star." *Sports Illustrated* 99, no. 3 (July 28, 2003).

McNeil, David. "Sexy and Smart: One Sector That Won't Be Left Behind: Japan's Massive Sex Industry Has Shifted from Bricks-and-Mortar Deflation to Internet Elation." *Japan, Inc.,* September 2003.

Morris, M. "Telling Tails Explain the Discrepancy in Sexual Partner Reports." *Nature* 365 (September 30, 1993): 437–40.

Niehaus, Isak. "Biographical Lessons: Life Stories, Sex and Culture in Bushbuckridge, South Africa." *Cahiers d'études africaines* 181 (2006).

Ollivier, Debra. "France vs. America: The Sex Front." Salon.com, June 20, 2003.

Ortiz, Steven M. "Traveling with the Ball Club: A Code of Conduct for Wives Only." *Symbolic Interaction* 2, no. 3 (1997): 225–49.

Oster, Emily. "HIV and Sexual Behavior Change: Why Not Africa?" Working paper, National Bureau of Economic Research.

Oster, Emily, and William L. Parish. "Sexual Partners in China: Risk Patterns for Infection by HIV and Possible Interventions," in *Social Policy and HIV/AIDS in China.* Joan Kaufman et al., eds. Cambridge, MA: Harvard University Press, 2006.

Pao, Maureen. "Hello Shanghai: One China, Two Wives." *Far Eastern Economic Review,* July 5, 2001.

Pettifor, A. E., H. V. Rees, I. Kleinschmidt, et al. "Young People's Sexual Health in South Africa: HIV Prevalence and Sexual Behaviors from a Nationally Representative Household Survey." *AIDS* 19, no. 14 (September 23, 2005): 1525–34.

Robert-Diard, Pascale. "François Mitterrand A Été Inhumé dans Sa Ville Natale." *Le Monde,* January 13, 1996.

Schmitt, David, and 121 members of the ISDP. "Patterns and Universals of Mate Poaching Across 53 Nations." *Journal of Personality and Social Psychology* 86 no. 4 (2004): 560–84.

Sciolino, Elaine. "Paris Journal; A Tell-All's Tale: French Politicians Stray Early and Often." *New York Times,* October 17, 2006.

Shelton, J. D., Daniel Halperin, Vinand Nantulya, Malcolm Potts, Helene D. Gayle, and King K. Holmes. "Partner Reduction Is Crucial for Balanced 'ABC' Approach to HIV Prevention." *BMJ* 328 (April 10, 2004).

Slaymaker, Emma, and Martine Collumbien, personal communication.

Spanier, Graham B., and Randie L. Margolis. "Marital Separation and Extramarital Sexual Behavior." *Journal of Sex Research* 19 (1983): 23–48.

Spector, Michael. "The Devastation." *New Yorker,* October 11, 2004.

Stadler, Jonathan. "The Young, the Rich, and the Beautiful: Secrecy, Suspicion and Discourses of AIDS in the South African Lowveld."

African Journal of AIDS Research 2, no. 2 (November 1, 2003): 127–39(13).

———. "Rumor, Gossip and Blame: Implications for HIV/AIDS Prevention in the South African Lowveld." *AIDS Education and Prevention* 15, no. 4, 357–68, 2003.

Stoneburner, Rand L., and Daniel Low-Beer. "Population-Level HIV Declines and Behavioral Risk Avoidance in Uganda." *Science* 304 (April 30, 2004).

Talbot, David. "This Hypocrite Broke Up My Family." Salon.com, September 16, 1998.

Tam, Siumi Maria. "Normalization of "Second Wives": Gender Contestation in Hong Kong." *Asian Journal of Women's Studies* 2 (1996): 113–32.

Thomson, Alice. "Labour Is in No Position to Preach to Us About Respect." opinion.telegraph, November 1, 2005.

Tran, Lisa. "Concubines Under Modern Chinese Law." Ph.D. dissertatno, UCLA, 2005.

Treas, Judith, and Deirdre Giesen. "Sexual Infidelity Among Married and Cohabiting Americans." *Journal of Marriage and the Family* 62 (2000): 48–60.

Trueheart, Charles. "Waiting for Sarko." *Atlantic Monthly,* September 2005.

Watts, Jonathan. "China Tries to Stem Soaring Divorce Rate." *Guardian,* March 2, 2005.

Widmer, Eric D., Judith Treas, and Robert Newcomb. "Attitudes Toward Nonmarital Sex in Twenty-four Countries." *Journal of Sex Research* 35, no. 4 (November 1998).

Wiederman, Michael. "Extramarital Sex: Prevalence and Correlattes in a National Survey." *Journal of Sex Research* 34 (1997): 167–74.

Williams, B., et al. "Changing Patterns of Knowledge, Reported Behaviour and Sexually Transmitted Infections in a South African Gold Mining Community." *AIDS* 17 (2003): 2009–17.

Willsher, Kim. "Ordeal of Elysée's Hidden Daughter." *Guardian,* February 25, 2005.

Wiseman, Paul. "Cheating Is Big Business for Chinese Private Eyes." *USA Today,* April 15, 2005.

Yardley, Jim. "Women in China Embrace Divorce as Stigma Eases." *New York Times,* October 4, 2005.

Zha Bo and Geng Wenxiu. "Sexuality in Urban China." *Australian Journal of Chinese Affairs* 28 (July 1992).

"Hyde Summation," January 16, 1999, transcribed by Federal Document Clearing House, Washingtonpost.com.

"Judiciary Committee Unveils Four Articles of Impeachment." CNN.com, December 9, 1998.

"Clinton Apologizes Again for His Conduct." CNN.com, September 9, 1998.

"Among Wealthy Nations U.S. Stands Alone in Its Embrace of Religion." Pew Global Attitudes Project, December 19, 2002.

WEB SITES

General Social Survey of the National Opinion Research Center, University of Chicago.

CIA—The World Factbook, https://wwwcia.gov/cia/publications/factbook/index.html

The Gay Men's Health Crisis HIV/AIDS Timeline, http://www.gmhc.org/about/timeline.html

The Gallup Organization, Moral Issues, poll conducted May 8–11, 2006. www.galluppoll.com